Unearthing My Religion

Real Talk about Real Faith

Mary Gray-Reeves

Morehouse Publishing
NEW YORK · HARRISBURG · DENVER

Copyright © 2013 by Mary Gray-Reeves

All rights reserved. No part of this book may be reproduced, stored in a retrieval system, or transmitted in any form or by any means, electronic or mechanical, including photocopying, recording, or otherwise, without the written permission of the publisher.

Unless otherwise noted, the Scripture quotations contained herein are from the New Revised Standard Version Bible, copyright © 1989 by the Division of Christian Education of the National Council of Churches of Christ in the U.S.A. Used by permission. All rights reserved.

Morehouse Publishing, 4775 Linglestown Road, Harrisburg, PA 17112
Morehouse Publishing, 19 East 34th Street, New York, NY 10016
Morehouse Publishing is an imprint of Church Publishing Incorporated.

www.churchpublishing.org

Cover design by Laurie Klein Westhafer
Typeset by Denise Hoff

Library of Congress Cataloging-in-Publication Data
Gray-Reeves, Mary.
   Unearthing my religion : real talk about real faith / Mary Gray-Reeves.
      pages cm
   Includes bibliographical references.
   ISBN 978-0-8192-2887-1 (pbk.) -- ISBN 978-0-8192-2888-8
(ebook) 1. Apologetics. 2. Theology. 3. Spirituality--Christianity.
4. Spiritual life--Christianity. I. Title.
   BT1103.G73 2013
   230--dc23

                              2013018534

Printed in the United States of America

*With gratitude and love to
Michael, Katie, and Dorian
through whom I have learned so much
about receiving and giving grace,
and to Paul Edwards,
faithful priest, mentor, and friend,
who thankfully speaks of grace
even more than I do!*

CONTENTS

Everybody Has a Story

If you picked up this book, then you might agree that our lives are guided, at least in part, by spirit. In reading this simple volume, I hope you will discover something deeper of your spirit and how it connects to your daily life and the wider world. I hope the story of your life can be rooted in a spiritual home, a wider community in which you live the story.

The consciousness of my spiritual story happened to begin in a religious place: church.

I regularly helped my mother with her altar guild tasks, which involved cleaning and preparing the church for Sunday worship. In The Episcopal Church at that time, girls could not serve at the altar during worship, but I could be at the altar with my mother doing this "women's work."

I was age five or six when I was given the job of washing the large marble altar—I suppose because you couldn't move it, knock it over, or otherwise destroy it. I loved washing the massive table at which mystical things seemed to occur. I moved around it and under it, wiping every inch. Sometimes, resting from my task, I lay on my back looking up at the marble pattern of its underbelly, illumined by sunlight coming through windows nearby. There I communed with God, not in the formal, structured worship of Sunday morning, but engaged in wonder and enjoyment with God who was playmate and friend. This was the place I learned to worship; that is, to offer a genuine response to God's presence. I did not intellectually "believe" anything, yet every fiber of my being was open to God. These encounters drew me into the sacred mystery and began a lifelong companionship with the holy.

Church is still the place I call my spiritual home and the place I still live my story. This includes wrestling with life's big questions just as most people do. The solid spiritual foundation that has me sometimes resting, and sometimes wrestling, was formed in those first wordless encounters. They pulsed into my being the deep knowledge of God's abiding love and grace that gives me life. Even now, when my faith becomes too rational, or when life seems less than solid, I remember to dwell in wonder and mystery once again. Playful enjoyment with the divine is a wonderful teacher of grace and a strong foundation on which to build a spiritual life.

Spiritual *and* Religious

I was on a plane recently with someone who turned out to be a religious writer. As our conversation got underway, I asked her, "Are you a Christian?" She replied, "It depends on what you mean by that."

Once upon a time, people sought the answers to life's big questions from religion, the dispenser of truth. A "religious experience" was generally understood to mean a "spiritual experience"; one was at home with the other. As the woman on the plane proved, these two words are no longer synonymous. Robert Fuller distinguishes the words thus:

The popular definitions of the words diverged throughout the twentieth century: The word *spiritual* gradually came to be associated with the private realm of thought and experience, while the word *religious* came to be connected with the public realm of membership in religious institutions, participation in formal ritual, and adherence to official denominational doctrines. Not only did the words come to signify different aspects of faith by the early twenty-first century, but the terms "spiritual" and "religious" have become laden with emotional connotations. In general, "spirituality" is taken as a positive term, whereas "religion" is often negative; spirituality is understood as somehow more authentic, religion as having "a somewhat cynical orientation."[1]

In fact, the research reflects that people who at one time said they were "religious only" now identify as "spiritual *and* religious," as opposed to one or another. Diana Butler Bass in *Christianity After Religion: The End of Church and the Birth of a New Spiritual Awakening* surmises that people who participate in religious practice are increasingly dissatisfied with their experience, but continue to express spiritual longing.[2] Even religious people have abandoned the understanding that spirituality and religion should be measured together. Increasingly, we move through religious life buffet style—that is, we exercise spiritual freedom by choosing a relative position to a religious institutional practice or belief. We might accept its doctrines wholeheartedly, conditionally, skeptically, or not at all. It is up to us.

---

1 As quoted in Diana Butler Bass, *Christianity After Religion: The End of Church and the Birth of a New Spiritual Awakening* (New York: Harper One, 2012), 67.

2 Ibid, 91–94. Bass discusses the important category of "spiritual and religious" and its relation to various faith traditions, not just Christianity.

There are any number of reasons why so many Americans find much of organized religion incapable of touching their personal, spiritual lives. Many do not find a place in religion to express their voice. Religious institutions may not allow individuals to exercise personal power. They may function in hierarchical ways where some get to speak and others do not. Religious organizations have sometimes grown isolated from their communities as institutional decline encroaches.

There exists, however, a vast space between mindless institutional participation and extreme individualism that fears a loss of personal power through religious involvement. This book seeks to help create a fertile meeting ground of conversation somewhere between the two.

The Space Between

I am both spiritual *and* religious. I have an active personal inner life and I am a public part of organized religion. I am a Christian, to be specific. I am Episcopalian, to be even more precise. I qualify in the eyes of many as *really* religious, since I am a bishop in The Episcopal Church. As such, I inhabit an iconic position; one that has historic and global connections to the wider church, both geographically and across history.[3]

My commitment to the church does not mean I lack dialogue with God, my faith beliefs, or my institution. Conversation, including argument, is an essential part of spirituality, of the faith life, both private and public. If I were not part of an organized religion, I would still be spiritual. I would still explore my inner life. But as someone who is "spiritual and religious," being in relationship with others is part of the process of deepening my life with God. It is the place, for me, where holy companionship is acknowledged, enhanced, and shared.

---

3 In The Episcopal Church both women and men may be ordained deacons, priests, and bishops, married and have families. The expectations, vows, and ordination ritual for the ministry of bishop may be found in The Book of Common Prayer, 512–23.

As both "spiritual and religious," I am apparently in the fastest growing category of Americans with regard to spiritual and religious life.[4] We are in the broad and large middle of the religious landscape alongside the growing group of those who define themselves as "unaffiliated" and "spiritual but not religious." If we think about these categories on a spectrum, the farthest ends would include those who are "religious only" and those who claim "nothing."

The middle has in common a desire to grow spiritually and is not averse to gathering in community. Would it be possible for religious institutions to become places of spiritual dialogue? Locations where people on the entire "spiritual and/or religious" spectrum could gather for meaningful engagement with God and one another? Could people develop greater articulation about what exactly they mean when they use that word, "spiritual"? Instead of avoiding conversations about our civic and spiritual life, we could intentionally create space for it, perhaps discovering satisfaction for the spiritual longing of both individual and society. What might such a gathering look like in your religious organization? In your neighborhood? Who might come? Would you attend?

In this age of transition, religious organizations have a rich spiritual inheritance that often spans thousands of years. We have an opportunity to more widely open our spaces, physically, linguistically, and culturally. We could create hospitable space for dialogue with those who have spiritual lives different from our own. We could discover and create language between us. We might achieve deeper understanding of the fullness of the spiritual/religious spectrum. Maybe we could send spiritual energy, love, and grace into our communities, and rise above difference for the common good. Interfaith or interreligious dialogue is a great place to start. The problems of our world could use our collective wisdom.

---

4   Bass, ibid, on pgs 91-94 argues that survey data reflects rapid and substantial growth in a desire for spirituality among religious people in America.

What Words Shall We Use?

Creating open and accessible space for the sharing of diverse gifts will require effort. Despite America's expanse of cultural diversity, we typically still enjoy enclaves of sameness. Our cultural realities, the worlds in which we live day-to-day, all have their own language. While we live in a more or less common land, we speak differently across race, nation of origin, social and economic class, religious identity, gender, age, and professional cultures.

We continue to have segregated conversations on things of the spirit. It is hard work to carefully consider one's choice of words to meet the understanding of a listener, refrain from inside expressions or sayings, and use one's face and body language to encourage communication and workable bonds. If you have ever had to communicate in a language not your first, then you know the experience.

For institutions to create space for dialogue among diversity, a strong sense of identity that includes the capacity for inclusion makes a difference. As institutions, if we speak only to ourselves, and are concerned only about institutional survival, then we will need to change. Such a mindset will not serve us for long.

Language is changing in culture all the time. I am a fan of Stephen Colbert. In particular, I find intriguing his "Tonight's Word" segment, where he puts a new contextual spin on a universally defined word. A master of the double entendre, he banters with his guests and viewers—the "Colbert Nation"—as together they explore how we will speak in our country today.

I hope this book will similarly inspire the reader to engage well-known words afresh, so that you and those with whom you dialogue might become more thoughtful and spiritually expressive. I hope you as reader will argue with what I say, change it up, and find your own local and indigenous expression of spiritual and faith language. I hope what I write helps you to become a more articulate communicator of your spiritual story, and if you have one, that of your faith tradition. Everyone has a story, and each one is powerful and compelling in its own way.

In my own efforts to embody the spirit of dialogue in this book, I have sought to be as uncomplicated in my use of words as possible, avoiding heavy religious language and explaining it when I do. For the religiously eloquent, there is nothing terribly academic in these chapters. If you are a seasoned Christian, you will wonder why you are reading this book. The truth is, often those of us who have lived the faith awhile have a difficult time explaining why we believe what we believe or sharing spiritual experiences. Often we spend most of our time speaking to people like ourselves. We just assume others know what we are talking about, that everyone lives spiritually as we live.

In today's world, they do not. If what I have written seems incredibly basic, it may be that my articulation of spirituality and faith can help the seasoned Christian speak with less complexity to those who are just beginning to explore the spiritual or faith life. For the person just starting to articulate their spiritual story, I pray that I have managed to use everyday words that will direct the heart, mind, and spirit into a deeper experience of spirituality, regardless of religious background.[5]

People over the years have told me I am capable of explaining faith in ways that are comprehensible for a wide range of individuals. Things I say apparently help them explore their spiritual lives and connection with God. I have not gained that proficiency by talking to myself, but being in conversation with others. Accordingly, while you can read this book on your own, engaging its content with other people will enhance and deepen your experience. Communities, whether short or long term, are where the "rubber meets the road" of spiritual growth. Being in one can make all the difference to the journey. In addition then to developing language to articulate your spiritual story, I hope these words will help diverse groups of people to gather, read,

---

5 One disclaimer: this book does reflect a Christian-liberal-Episcopal perspective and leans toward that religious and spiritual identity.

and talk about the spiritual life, learning and growing together as community.

This book will address six basic words used in Christian faith: **spirituality, grace, faith, worship, community,** and **religion**. These words are of primary relevance to those already involved in a life of faith, but they can also be points of entry for those new to spiritual exploration and Christianity. The order of the words also mirrors the way most people come into the Christian life today. The average person who is seeking spirituality or a faith life does not begin with organized religion. They begin with spiritual longing of some sort. If we are going to have real talk about faith, it does not necessarily begin with religion.

In particular you will notice that, in addition to a chapter on grace, I use the word "grace" a lot. Anyone who spends time with me will tell you this. I am passionate about helping people put the concept of grace—by which I mean the unconditional and unearned favor of God—to use in their lives.[6] Discovering the grace of God is a powerful catalyst for living well spiritually. It remains my deepest honor to accompany people—and be accompanied—on a journey of grace; to experience together key insights, transformation, and forward movement as we awaken to its very simple yet profound reality.

It is my hope that seasoned Christians and those searching for something yet unknown to them will find deeper knowledge of God here, not by thinking *about* God or grace, so much as by *experiencing* God and grace and turning these words into daily spiritual practice. In my opinion, when we "unearth" the religion of Christianity, what we find is grace. It is at the heart of all things Christian. That said, it must be noted that grace is not confined to Christianity. That would make it conditional, and grace is not. It is free, it is a gift, and it can be anywhere in anyone.

---

6 In short, grace is "God's favor towards us [humanity], unearned and undeserved" (The Book of Common Prayer, 858). Experiencing God's presence and grace is a spiritual practice.

Besides grace, each of the six words I explore here will have a simple explanation, a simple spiritual practice, some wondering questions, and a link to the Bible through an agricultural parable or metaphor attributed to Jesus.[7] I have used these particular words of Jesus because they are accessible, but also because they are foundational to Christian spiritual and religious practice. Jesus taught deep things of God using everyday examples everyone could understand. That is clear in these parables.

Certainly the Bible is rooted in particular times and places. But the vocabulary of food, soil, seeds, weeds, pruning, labor, and family farming are experiences that many of us can still understand. Even if you don't know about farming, everyone eats food. As Jesus knew, such simple everyday things make for comprehensible, spiritual metaphor that can be used anywhere by anyone. It is usually the simplest of truths in life that take root and ground us.

I live on the central coast of California in what is known as the "Salad Bowl of America." Due to the unique and varied soil and climate conditions, most of the country's lettuce and spinach is grown in this region, as are many other crops. Large- and small-scale agriculture has a significant base here, even if the actual growing happens in other parts of the country.

I have spent time with local farmers and learned something of how they think and see the world. Growing our nation's food is both vocation and passion, and not just a job. I have been richly blessed by the spiritual connections farmers make when planting seeds, nurturing them to fruition and harvesting them. I am no expert, but expertise is not required for the natural world to teach us something of the spiritual life. I have included

---

7 The use of "spiritual practice" has become even more widespread in this day through the emerging church movement. The systematized practice of disciplines such as prayer and study and physical activities such as fasting have been used for thousands of years by many religions. While certain practices are linked to certain traditions, there is no reason one cannot refer to a wide range of deepening and enlightening spiritual habits as a spiritual practice.

farmer's words and stories in order to "earth" the words of Jesus in our own daily reality of feeding ourselves physical food. This will enhance the spiritual power of Jesus's words and thereby increase our own spiritual nutritional intake. The accessibility of his words will also teach us how to speak about the spiritual life and faith with greater ease and simplicity.

With Gratitude

I would like to thank all those involved in the enterprise of farming for putting beautiful and nutritious food on American tables every day, particularly Bruce Taylor, Tanya Mason, and Albert Garnica of Taylor Farms; Dirk Gianinni and Ricardo Reyes of Christensen and Gianinni Farms; Robin Denney for her tutelage on pruning grape vines; and Stephen Pessagno and Robin Dodd of Pessagno Winery. They made time, expertise, land, and their passion for farming available to me for the writing of this book—and for the growth of my own spiritual life. Thank you.

Finally, I would like to thank the many Christians with whom I have shared faith community throughout my life, people who have taught me so much about the loving God I know through Jesus and his grace. You have accompanied me through numerous transformations, and I am blessed by our common journey. I am also thankful for my friends who are not Christian, or of any faith, with whom I also have fruitful and transforming relationships. You have taught me how to speak about faith—and how not to. And to Stephanie Spellers, my editor, my taskmaster, and my friend; this process of writing has been a deep blessing in my life and I am ever grateful. Finally, to the Holy One, I am indebted with my life for such deep love, faithfulness, and holy companionship.

CHAPTER 1

Spirituality Is the Experience, Noticing Is the Practice

"Every day I listen to the dirt. What are you telling me? What do you need? What do you want to give?"

—*Dirk Gianinni, fourth-generation farmer in Salinas, California*

Maybe I Really Am the Center of the Universe

Spirituality is a commonly used word these days, and it has many different meanings and perspectives. If you google "spirituality" without any further definition, you will get nearly 100 million references. Christian spirituality brings 5.6 million results; Sufi spirituality, 4 million; Buddhist spirituality, 8 million; Hindu spirituality, 12 million; and so on. It is a topic of some interest.

While definition and use vary, we can safely say that spirituality is something about having an experience beyond ourselves, within ourselves. It is a connection with an entity beyond our personal reality of heart, body, and mind. Whether we call this other reality God, or this "other" is some aspect of the creation or even solitude, we seem to yearn for connection outside ourselves.

As we noted in the introduction, spirituality has not always been the purview of the individual. All cultures throughout time have valued some sort of spiritual experience as part of the framework for their common life. Historically, organized religion has been the place for integrating the development of an inner life, community, and service to humankind. Most cultures would have understood these as part and parcel of one another. But they are now increasingly segregated. Harvey Cox shares these thoughts on the increased interest in spirituality apart from religion:

> "Spirituality" can mean a host of things, but there are three reasons why the term is in such wide use. First, it is still a form of tacit protest. It reflects a widespread discontent with the

preshrinking of "religion," Christianity in particular, into a package of theological propositions by the religious corporations that box and
distribute such packages. Second, it represents
an attempt to voice the awe and wonder before
the intricacy of nature that many feel is essential
to human life without stuffing them into ready-
to-wear ecclesiastical patterns. Third, it recog-
nizes the increasingly porous borders between
the different traditions and, like the early Christian movement, it looks more to the future than
to the past.[8]

As a spiritual and religious leader, I would add to Cox's com-
ments. Deep in the American cultural DNA is the inalienable
right to pursue happiness. This is a founding principle, one of
our non-negotiables. I wonder if this conviction has evolved over
time to mean that if we are not happy and personally pleased
with life, then we are being denied the right to be fully who we
determine ourselves to be. More communally minded cultures do
not place the same value on personal happiness and satisfaction
that we do. Ancient spiritual practices originated in these kinds
of highly communal contexts, but the American quest seems to
have disconnected spirituality from its roots and reframed it as
part of our individual pursuit of happiness. The conflict comes
when we want a community's spiritual offering, but do not want
the accountability that being in community usually involves.

As I write, Arianna Huffington (whose online news outlet
The Huffington Post hosts some of the most important religious and social conversations in America) is working with app
wonks on creating "GPS for the Soul," so that with a brush of
the finger, a person can come back to his or her inner center
after having veered away. On the current website there are many
ideas, personal stories, and encouraging words, not necessarily
religious or connected to a divine energy beyond ourselves. They

8 Harvey Cox, *The Future of Faith* (New York: Harper-Collins, 2009), 13.

are intended to reconnect a person to "that place" within where we find peace and a clear sense of self. Huffington notes her original hope: "That one day someone would create an app that would gauge the state of your mind, body, and spirit, then automatically offer the exact steps you would need to take to realign all three aspects of your being."[9] I will leave the reader to ponder this next electronic solution to all of life's challenges. But if it were just a matter of reading an idea perfectly tailored for one's spiritual make-up to regroup the grounding of the soul, why are we still searching?

Our American mindset pursues happiness and we think we can buy it. Yet the most grounded and wise spiritual teachers and practitioners usually have the least amount of stuff and are not typically looking up spiritual wellness on their smartphones. But for the average American, the practice of spirituality, in its most primal form, has come to mean the individual pursuit of happiness, of feeling better through various self-selected mental and physical practices, not necessarily connected to other people, a religious tradition, or even a divine power.

Spirituality has come to include any and all self-stylized options for a pleasurable inner experience, stress-reduction, or mental clarity. It is sometimes a means to an end, rather than a way of being in touch with eternal things. More deeply, though, perhaps it is a yearning for the reintegration of self, others, and service to humankind, or the discovery of one's purpose in life. While extreme individualism seems philosophically ideal, it does not always work out practically.

It is helpful to be aware of why spirituality personally interests us. What do we hope to gain by developing the inner life? If we are not clear on this question, we run the risk of perpetuating our dissatisfaction by not committing deeply, at least for a time, to a single spiritual way or practice. Commitment in and of itself bears the fruit of spiritual depth and inner peace. The pursuit

---

9 http://www.huffingtonpost.com/gps-for-the-soul

of spirituality can, however, become like any other addiction: something we pursue for the high it delivers in a given moment.

The Spiritual Practice of Noticing

A meaningful spiritual experience that can become a spiritual practice is "noticing." It is a simple concept, I know. Yet how often do we move through life not noticing much at all? If we wish to move beyond a temporary good feeling that leads to ultimate joy despite life circumstances, we must begin with where we find ourselves. And so the first step is to simply notice yourself.

If you are unhappy, acknowledge it. Often in our efforts to feel better, we run to the next thing, trying to get away from the experience of feeling bad. If you are content, pay attention to that too. Noticing, elevated to the level of spiritual practice, helps us hold still and take stock of where we are. The earliest experiences of this practice only need to be momentary. When you are ready, you can begin to sit for longer periods, noticing thoughts and feelings. Practice noticing your thoughts and feelings each morning and evening. Move from there to noticing your surroundings and how they affect you. Both our inner and outer environment make a difference to our experience of life.

If we have previously been running away from ourselves, wanting to be anywhere but in our own lives, the first fruit of the practice of noticing is awareness that whatever we have been doing to find satisfaction is not working. This is a very important harvest, even if it feels small. Such an acknowledgment precedes any future change we might make. We cannot discover where we are going if we do not first know where we are. We cannot grow something new in our lives if we are not first willing to acknowledge the condition in which we find ourselves.

If we are blaming conditions or people for our unhappiness, until we notice ourselves we will not release them from culpability. Others are not responsible for our inner peace. If our choice is to "feel better," to pursue joy through spirituality, such transformation begins inside our own soul, not outside with blame of another person or life circumstance.

Soul and Spirit

There is a vast array of philosophical writing on matters of the self, the spirit, and the soul. Our view of them is culturally influenced. In the West, we tend to use these words interchangeably in our everyday cultural language. I would like to differentiate them even if only briefly and simplistically.

When I speak of the soul, I mean the very heart of who we are, that which may extend beyond our corporeal selves. The soul connects our deepest self to the self of all else. It is our essence. Some would say our soul is connected to eternity. When we speak of "soul mates," for instance, we are communicating that a particular relationship touches and shapes us at the deepest level of who we are. When we speak of soulful language or music, we are speaking of genuine and heartfelt expressions from the core of someone's being, artfully made known through the disciplined engagement of that person's spirit.

Our spirit is expressed as the synchronistic engagement of mind, heart, and will, through which we become more conscious of and strengthen our connection to the soul. Think of the spirit as a muscle. We can experience greater well-being and grounding that brings deeper contentment and self-understanding when we exercise our spirit. Spiritual practices mobilize the spirit for its proper use of knowing the unseen realities of life. It can be either strong and healthy or underutilized and inefficient, contributing little to the strength of our being. When we use the word "self" with "spirit" and "soul," we are referring to intertwined intangible realities that are part of who we are, and which make up a healthy spiritual system (like any important physiological system) that keeps us living well in the world.

Some religions understand the soul as eternal, or at least connected to the eternal, which has no beginning or end. In this understanding of soul and spirit, one assumes the presence of another entity, God, an energy or a ground that connects all being. It is a distinct reality, with which we can be united, and which has the power to transform us. This understanding of the spiritual quest beckons our engagement of something other than ourselves. We experience that it really isn't just about us, and that synergy with the other makes us fully alive.

The Dream of a Common Language

With the decline of Christianity as the primary faith in America, we have also lost a common language with which to convey spiritual truths in the wider culture. Remembering Cox's quote, perhaps if Christianity had focused less on the "packaging of theological propositions," we might be more of a resource to people seeking spiritual conversation today. Religions do hold valuable truths, grounded in ancient faith tradition that would prove helpful to the spiritual quest of Americans. Without those roots, many of us lack spiritual language that could be helpful to develop our inner spiritual lives.

Consider the story of the birth of Jesus. Americans celebrate this event at Christmas as a secular expression of gratitude, family, and gift-giving. More deeply, Christians celebrate in awe and wonder that God is not separate from people's lives, but in Christ, God dwells and lives fully with us. We use the word "incarnation" to express that in Jesus, God is made known, "enfleshed," so that humanity can have something tangible through which we might experience the fullness of God.

Whether the story of the birth of Jesus to Mary and Joseph in Bethlehem is historically accurate is less relevant to our spiritual growth than the knowledge that as we seek to draw closer to God, God has already drawn close to us. The story behind the holiday of Christmas celebrates a spiritual truth that opens the heart and mind to the idea that a divine entity outside of ourselves may be interested in a relationship with us.

That is one way a religion helps to deepen spiritual awareness. Jesus himself is another. He was a first-century Palestinian rabbi, a spiritual teacher. He spoke often in stories, parables, and metaphors, using everyday things to convey spiritual truths that would enrich people's understanding of God. He empowered the synergism between human and divine.

The life of Jesus was very specifically and intentionally about revealing God and helping people draw close to God. This was his human purpose. While Christian doctrine understands Jesus's identity in a particular way (savior, messiah, son of God), he could also be viewed as a metaphor for God: a story who in his person conveys God. In *The Power of Parable: How Fiction by Jesus Became Fiction about Jesus*, John Dominic Crossan defines the relationship between parable and metaphor in this way:

> A parable . . . is a metaphor expanded into a story, or, more simply, *a parable is a metaphorical story.* But what is a metaphor, what is a story, and how does their combination as metaphorical story differ from any other type of story—from, say, the novel you have just read or the film you have just seen? The term "metaphor" comes from two Greek roots; one is *meta,* "over" or "across," and the other *pherein,* "to bear" or "to carry." Metaphor means "carrying something over" from one thing to another and thereby "seeing something as another" or "speaking of something as another." . . . [A] parable, that is, a metaphorical story, always points externally beyond itself, points to some different and much wider referent.[10]

To see meaning beyond the simple details of parables or metaphors, you must be willing to be "carried across" to something deeper than what at first might appear. If you remain only

<hr>

10 John Dominic Crossan, *The Power of Parable: How Fiction by Jesus Became Fiction about Jesus* (New York: Harper One, 2012), 7-8.

at the level of story, or the details of historical accuracy, then you miss, or worse, avoid deeper spiritual truth. Every word Jesus spoke was meant to facilitate the connection between God and humanity and to create community around that union.

Returning to our spiritual practice of "noticing," a parable that might be useful is the Parable of the Sower (found in the Gospel of Luke 8:4–15, also in the Gospels of Matthew 13:1–23 and Mark 4:2–20, all three slightly different from one another).

Jesus spoke these words. Sit with them for awhile.

> When a great crowd gathered and people from town after town came to him, he said in a parable: "A sower went out to sow his seed; and as he sowed, some fell on the path and was trampled on, and the birds of the air ate it up. Some fell on the rock; and as it grew up, it withered for lack of moisture. Some fell among thorns, and the thorns grew with it and choked it. Some fell into good soil, and when it grew, it produced a hundredfold." As he said this, he called out, "Let anyone with ears to hear listen!"
>
> Then his disciples asked him what this parable meant. He said, "To you it has been given to know the secrets of the kingdom of God; but to others I speak in parables, so that 'looking they may not perceive, and listening they may not understand.'
>
> **The Parable of the Sower Explained**
> "Now the parable is this: The seed is the word of God. The ones on the path are those who have heard; then the devil comes and takes away the word from their hearts, so that they may not believe and be saved. The ones on the rock are those who, when they hear the word, receive it with joy. But these have no root; they believe

only for a while and in a time of testing fall
away. As for what fell among the thorns, these
are the ones who hear; but as they go on their
way, they are choked by the cares and riches and
pleasures of life, and their fruit does not mature.
But as for that in the good soil, these are the
ones who, when they hear the word, hold it fast
in an honest and good heart, and bear fruit with
patient endurance." (Luke 8:4–15)

I am not a farmer, but I admire and appreciate them. They
possess skill, knowledge, wisdom, and intuition honed over
many seasons. In both small and large enterprises, I am always
impressed that farmers are so mindful of the constant play
between weather, viruses, mold, bugs, weeds, economy, labor
force, market demand, and soil.

I often drive the 101 freeway, the major artery running north
and south the length of California. In the region where I live, it
runs for miles through fields where all sorts of fruits and vegetables are grown. I am now accustomed to watching the growth,
development, and harvest of various crops at different times of
the year. When driving with others at seventy miles per hour,
we play "Name That Crop!" The rhythm of a regular growing
cycle is clearer to me now, and I notice when weather or other
circumstances force humans to adjust accordingly, speeding up
or delaying a harvest. Everyone is paying attention and making
daily shifts to their lives. Farmers elevate the practice of noticing
to an art form. Noticing farmers and thinking of them as metaphor has helped my own spiritual practice and made me more
conscious of the subtle shifts in my inner life and surrounding
environment.

In my early observations, I sometimes would see a lone
person standing in a dirt field, not yet planted (as far as I could
tell), just staring down at the ground. I was intrigued by these
sightings, wondering what in the world they were looking at.
I decided one day to take a walk along a road next to a dirt

field, with no plant yet emerging. I stood and stared at the dirt as farmers do. I wanted to see what they see, but I just saw dirt. Untrained as I was, I imagined there must be all sorts of life in the soil and I was curious to know more. I knew it was capable of producing food, of sustaining life, even though like most Americans I interacted primarily with food via the grocery store. I could not assess the soil by its color, nor did I know if the nutrients, moisture, time of year, and other variables were right for growing a particular kind of food. While I could see it was dark and rich looking, it was in the end for me indiscernible from any other plot of dirt.

When farmers look at soil, they see a detailed future, a strategic plan, the economy, politics, immigration laws, and the cultural preferences of various groups. I know now that when they are staring at the soil, they see a whole universe and how the tiny seeds they cast will be part of it. Their persistent study and experienced practice of noticing the soil and all related factors makes the difference in the harvest.

Unlike America today, most people in first-century Palestine—Jesus's audience—were farmers. Everyone understood what happened when seed fell on rock, was not watered, or was choked by thorns. Certain conditions produced certain results. It only makes sense. Jesus spoke in parables, metaphorical stories, and common everyday language to help people consider their capacity and level of receptivity to the presence of the spiritual seeds that God was scattering in their soul. The story is not only about ground conditions, but "carries over" to the listeners' inner life. It invites us to ask: Are the seeds God is casting on our spiritual soil taking root? What kinds of seeds are they? What is the condition of your inner soil? Is there spiritual receptivity within you? Will holy seeds develop? What does harvest look like? Do you care?

These were questions people might have thought about sitting and listening to Jesus then and now. They are timeless queries.

Parables and Spiritual Practice

If we thought of our soul as soil, we might notice a few things about how we personally activate spiritual growth. We might notice that at different seasons in our lives or in certain environments, we are more or less receptive to the fertile presence of God. A spiritual seed may fall on resistance, or a failure to notice what God is giving us. We might be vulnerable or fragile, open to everything. We may not be able to discern what should be avoided, resisted, or nurtured. Notice the condition of your soul and the capacity of your spirit to engage your present inner reality.

Growing deep spiritual roots requires a commitment to noticing ourselves and making subtle yet intentional daily shifts in our engagement between spirit and soul. This requires patience—not a common human trait. Many people who came to hear Jesus probably wanted a quick fix as we do: a motivational speech or perhaps a spirituality website with the exact combination of resources to cure what ails us. Everyone wants to feel better. As with most things in life that result in real transformation, we have to invest more commitment and attention to bear good fruit. A spiritual experience can be hard, and not always pleasurable, work. Our greatest transformations can involve deep pain. Hopefully the pain deters our need to learn that particular life lesson again, but we are impatient and stubborn, so sometimes the painful lessons come around more than once.

Perhaps this is what Jesus meant by seeds falling on rock, amidst thorns, or "the devil snatching the seeds away." In such conditions, the "tender shoot will wither and die." Jesus's explanation of the parable suggests that these conditions are real. He is not shaming the listener but acknowledging that spiritual receptivity and growth require careful attention and discipline, and sometimes even making changes in the soil of our soul.

Parables are Jesus's way of noticing humanity. He is honest and realistic about God and about people. Spiritual seeds, which the story implies God casts with abandon (no farmer would cast seed without first preparing the soil for the greatest receptivity and the least waste), only take root and come to fullness in good soil where they "hold it fast in an honest and good heart, and bear fruit with patient endurance."

The conscious discipline of noticing and nurturing our good soil allows God's seed to take root. Developing our resistant areas to make them more receptive also increases the zones where God's seeds may flourish. Metaphorically, we might clear rocks and thorns, discovering more usable soil fit for spiritual harvest. We could develop wisdom to resist forces that would snatch away good seed. We could learn to persevere through life's ups and downs, having let seeds of patience and forbearance take root.

We can also learn our optimal growing conditions. Grapevines, for example, thrive in slightly rocky and sandy soil, planted on hillsides. The pebbly terrain that resisted producing broccoli is perfect for grapes. The spiritual practice of noticing will help us understand our spiritual landscape and teach us discernment about what can grow when, or not at all.

Like the weather, life conditions are often beyond our control. Farmers always have a contingency plan, and when that fails, they know how to let go because the forces of nature have overwhelmed their hard-fought efforts. This is farming knowledge, but it is also spiritual wisdom. Knowing our souls is like farmers knowing their fields and the environment in which they planted. Discovering and exercising our spiritual system is like a farmer who, year in year out, studies his dirt and its interaction with the world around it. Because of that attention, the farmer can bring forth a harvest. So can we.

Return to the Spiritual Practice of Noticing

The first step toward a deeper spiritual life is to simply notice yourself. In our efforts to feel better, we sometimes run to the next thing, trying to get away from the experience of feeling bad without examining where we are. Where you are miserable, pay attention. Where you are content, pay attention to that too. Noticing, elevated to the level of spiritual practice, helps us hold still and take stock of where we are. Practice noticing your thoughts and feelings each morning and evening. Move from there to noticing your surroundings and how they impact you. This need only take a few minutes each day.

Wondering Questions

Wondering is an essential spiritual skill. It opens and relaxes the mind to more possibilities than we can ever imagine. Remember wondering as a child? Once upon a time we wondered about everything. The world was a fascinating place. I remember wondering about anything and everything when I would lie in the grass, gazing up at the sky, watching the clouds. What is your favorite wondering memory?

Spend some wondering time about your soul and what you think spirituality is. What do you notice about your inner landscape?

Imagine God casting seeds in your soul with ridiculous abandon. Where are they landing? Where are they living? Where are they dying? Where are they growing with deep roots and becoming fruitful? In other words, what parts of your spiritual life are flourishing? What parts are struggling?

Where is there potentially more good soil for future planting? In other words, what are the conditions where you find you are able to spiritually come alive? How can you create those conditions more widely? What would the fruits be? How will you celebrate that harvest? Who can you share it with?

CHAPTER 2

Grace Is the Essence, Grace Is the Practice

One of these days because of government regulations and labor shortages caused by immigration and border issues, the food will rot in the ground. It will be devastating for those of us who live this process and American families will suffer.

—Every farmer interviewed

Grace is God's unmerited favor, acceptance, welcome, and love for us, a pure gift requiring no reciprocity. What do you think when you hear those words?

Jesus spoke these words. Sit with them for awhile.

> For the kingdom of heaven is like a landowner who went out early in the morning to hire laborers for his vineyard. After agreeing with the laborers for the usual daily wage, he sent them into his vineyard. When he went out about nine o'clock, he saw others standing idle in the marketplace; and he said to them, "You also go into the vineyard, and I will pay you whatever is right." So they went. When he went out again about noon and about three o'clock, he did the same. And about five o'clock he went out and found others standing around; and he said to them, "Why are you standing here idle all day?" They said to him, "Because no one has hired us." He said to them, "You also go into the vineyard."
>
> When evening came, the owner of the vineyard said to his manager, "Call the laborers and give them their pay, beginning with the last and then going to the first." When those hired about five o'clock came, each of them received the usual daily wage. Now when the first came, they thought they would receive more; but each of

them also received the usual daily wage. And when they received it, they grumbled against the landowner, saying, "These last worked only one hour, and you have made them equal to us who have borne the burden of the day and the scorching heat." But he replied to one of them, "Friend, I am doing you no wrong; did you not agree with me for the usual daily wage? Take what belongs to you and go; I choose to give to this last the same as I give to you. Am I not allowed to do what I choose with what belongs to me? Or are you envious because I am generous?" So the last will be first, and the first will be last. (Matthew 20:1–16)

Grace and Life Are Not Fair

In the first century everyone in a community participated in a harvest. The only goal the villagers had during those weeks was to get the fruit off the vine and into the press. A family, if not an entire village, depended on it. Grapes were an important crop. They could be grown in the hot, dry summer. They were offered for trade and provided wine, which was essential for major celebrations such as weddings (important occasions in first-century Palestine). The harvest of the fruit was the goal, the big picture, the larger perspective. There was no time for idleness or fairness. All that mattered was to get the job done before the fruit rotted, rodents ate it, or some other fate befell it. Should the weather shift, the work might go around the clock until the harvest was in and processed. The winepress kept cranking for as long as was needed. Perhaps in the parable this is why some workers were idle for a time and then brought in at the last minute to help complete the work.

When Arizona instituted immigration policies discouraging people from crossing the U.S./Mexico border for work, farmers of all sorts felt the sting. Rumor has it that many went to the border in the middle of the night, stealthily, competing for workers with increased wages, bonus plans, and car raffles, enticing them to cross the border for their much needed labor. As in the parable, the harvest is the first concern, and there is no room for complaint, idleness, fairness, or politics. The owner of a vineyard or a farm has responsibility for the whole operation: the resources, the timing, the workers. Ultimately, the decision and the end result falls to them.

People listening to the parable would have understood the priority of the harvest. Hearing Jesus's story, they may have thought, "Fairness matters every other time—except at harvest time!" They also would have understood the wider context within which Jesus spoke. People wanted to know about the end times, God's final harvest, if you will. Jesus was known to include a wide circle of people, and people probably wanted to know if it was truly all right for non-Jews to benefit from God's harvest. Should they be invited into the life, labor, and reward of God?

For Jews, being the people of God was a birthright, lived out in the community of Jews and through adherence to Jewish law. Jesus broke with that tradition by welcoming non-Jews and Jews alike to share his ministry. For some, this would have been unfair, an insult even, to those who spent their lives devoted to their faith and religious community. How can outsiders just come in at the last minute and be treated as people who have been working hard all along? We can understand that sort of resentment. Somewhere in life, we have experienced it. But for Jesus, the greater priority was harvesting the fruit of grace. He sowed seeds of it everywhere he went and with everyone whom he met. Fairness would have been less important than giving people access to grace.

Grace Just Is

When a writer friend of mine approached a publisher on my behalf about a book on grace (an idea which morphed into the book you are now reading), I was told that the publisher's response was, "Grace doesn't sell." As one who can be flip of tongue, I said, "That's kind of the point."

If grace is a new word or concept for you, the most important thing to understand is, you can't buy it or sell it, own it, earn it, charge for it, require it, demand it, barter, cheat, steal, manipulate, or bargain for it. Grace is acceptance, favor, welcome, and love that comes as a pure gift requiring no reciprocity. It is not warranted by one's good behavior, chosenness, or worthiness. You can only receive it, live in it, and give it away. It is available for the taking—and the offering—every second of every day. If we take the grape harvest as a metaphor for grace, it pays no attention to time, rules, or anyone's sense of justice. It just is.

Grace, like love, is unseen, but very real and meaningful in our lives. We don't really value or understand it until we experience it—or until we do *not* experience it. Grace is understood as air is understood: by taking it into our being—and also by being deprived of it. There is, after all, nothing like having *no* air to breathe to understand the value of air.

Grace is hard to grasp, but words are a good starting place. In common usage grace is defined as "simple elegance or refinement of movement, courteous goodwill, an attractively polite manner of behaving."[11] In Christian theological language, it is defined as "God's favor towards us, unearned and undeserved; by grace God forgives our sins, enlightens our minds, stirs our hearts, and strengthens our wills."[12] The first one is easier to get a hold of. We know grace when we see it. We decide from our own perspective what is graceful and what is not. Like discerning what is beautiful, it is in the eye of the beholder. But the theological definition—"God's favor towards us, unearned and undeserved; by grace God forgives our sins, enlightens our minds, stirs our hearts, and strengthens our wills"—that is harder to grasp. What is that, really? And what difference does it make in one's life?

11 Available at http://Oxforddictionaries.com/us/definition/American_english/grace.
12 The Book of Common Prayer, 858.

Tomes have been written on the topic, but in short, "unearned and undeserved" grace is understood to be unconditional favor. That is, we cannot earn it. It is not quantitative or qualitative. There is no scale by which it may be measured because it is always present. In Christian theology, grace is generally understood to have no beginning or end. It is eternal. There is never a little or a lot of grace; it just is.

Just like air, grace is so important we want to quantify it, but trying to define grace by our experience in fact reduces its meaning to fit our capacity for it, which is often limited. To develop a life of grace one must be open to expanding the spirit, heart, and mind to include its eternal nature. If you have ever practiced yoga, then you know what a difference it can make to notice your breathing. Eventually you learn to control your breath in moments of stress or exertion—this grows your tranquility and self-control. Noticing grace will eventually do the same for our mind, spirit, and body.

When we begin to truly practice grace, we exhibit traits associated with the word's common usage. Think of people you know who seem to experience deeply that they are unconditionally loved by something greater than themselves. They forgive their own foibles and great sins. They forgive others. They are spiritually elegant and there is a beauty about them. We look at them and wonder how they became that way. We cannot imagine it for ourselves. And yet, if it is grace, it is for everyone.

I could relay any number of times in my life when I did not experience God's grace. The most harrowing will be familiar to anyone who has worked in food hospitality: waitress nightmares. Google it—this is a real term. It is very common for people who wait tables to wake in the night (in their own kitchen, if they also sleepwalk), imagining putting on an apron and holding a plate or a pitcher of water. I waited tables in both bars and restaurants while in college. Not infrequently in my dreams I imagined arriving at work naked, began working, taking no time to find clothes, and then was constantly behind in getting orders out or spilling very tall glasses of daiquiris all over people (which did actually happen on occasion). These were my dreams, but they pointed to my deep fear that I could not keep up, measure up, or feel anything less than vulnerable most of the time.

I knew the technical definition of grace back then, since I grew up as a Christian. I could articulate an experience of grace when I had one. I could say, *"That* was a moment of grace!" But then that moment and I would part ways, and life would go back to what I called normal, a state with a distinct lack of grace (or "ungrace"). What I did not know was how to experience grace more often. That would have been helpful. It is helpful now. I have many more moments of grace than ungrace than I used to. I am so thankful for its unconditional, limitless reality. Oh, and please tip your server graciously.

Where Is Grace?

Grace can go anywhere and is not bound by anything. It originates in God, is shared by God, and reflects the essence of God. One could detach it from an origin, although scientifically, all energy emerges from somewhere or something and goes somewhere or into something. I think grace is an energy, and "God" is as good a word for its origin as any other.

Sometimes Christians believe we own grace because we experience it in Jesus and in reading the Bible. The Gospel of John notes that Jesus is "full of grace and truth" and "from his fullness we have all received grace upon grace" (John 1:14–16). Christians experience our relationship with Jesus Christ as the power that draws us into a deeper understanding of God and ourselves. We are called to follow in the way of Jesus, and grace is his way.

Rather than see Christianity's distinctive emphasis on grace as exclusive or superior, we could view our religious purpose and witness as a call to be stewards of grace. As followers of Jesus the Christ, we are to spiritually practice grace, making it real and present in our everyday lives and that of our communities.

Christians make their commitment through the ritual of baptism, and daily, both publicly and privately, submit to the grace of God.

Grace Is in You . . . Eternally

We think experiences of grace are random. It comes across in sayings like, "There but for the grace of God go I"—suggesting that, in a particular moment, God gives us grace, but then withholds it in other moments. I don't really like that God. That God seems capricious and does not resonate with the God I experience in Jesus, who seemed a steady flow of grace all the time. I have come to understand that grace is not random; I am.

This is an important insight that could affect the way we receive grace and the way we give it to others. When I accept my own inconsistency, I can stop blaming someone or something for my condition and begin to change it as much as I am able. Even when someone is injuring me in some way, I can endure such an experience with grace—or without it. I know from experience that even when I am moving through difficult and painful situations that are beyond my control, I am more fruitful "in grace" than "out of grace." I am calmer and more peaceful, more open to the wisdom and insight God makes available to me through grace. I am able to see the bigger picture, keeping the event relative to the fullness of life. I make better decisions. I negotiate such challenging life circumstances with greater ease accompanied by grace rather than alone. With the simple practice of noticing where we are with regards to grace in a given moment, we can begin to open ourselves to it once again.

In chapter 1, I said noticing is an effective spiritual practice that grows our awareness. Grace as a spiritual practice develops in us the qualities of spiritual elegance. When we notice graceful or grace-filled people, what do we admire in them? Things like unconditional love, forgiveness, patience, peace, joy, and the vision to see possibilities beyond our current circumstances.

Through practice we, too, can embody the attributes we associate with spiritually beautiful people.

Each time we notice the presence of grace, we are engaged in a spiritual discipline that develops our spiritual life. Just noticing grace in ourselves or someone else helps us become better acquainted with it. As we come to know grace, we begin to understand our presence in the eternal life of God. Not the afterlife, with which we often confuse eternal life, but the life and the energy that has no beginning and no end and that surrounds and fills us in each moment. Through the experience of grace, we grow more open to the fullness of God now, in the present, and become more spiritually elegant.

Such elegance may seem a long way off from your present condition. Spiritual greats make it look easy. They always seem in touch with the attributes of eternal life. They seem so grounded. They will tell you though that they did not just wake up one day in such a state. They practiced, made it a daily discipline to seek grace everywhere. Spiritual greats have challenges in life as we all do: they doubt, they fall, they get up. It is not true that there are some human beings who are spiritual and others who are not. We are all spiritual beings. All have capacity for spiritual growth. Everyone has experiences of grace. You do not need to be favored with any particular circumstance; you just need to be willing to practice being conscious of grace, until it takes hold in your spiritual soil, and is harvested in your real life.

The Spiritual Practice of Grace

Since it is true that one thing builds on another, once again, practice *noticing*. Notice what you are thinking about right now. As you notice where you are mentally for a minute or so, notice your surroundings and where you are physically. What do you notice is consuming your mental and emotional energy today? Is it something from the past, a worry of the future, a relationship or situation that is not going well? Is it a feeling about yourself or someone else? Does your brain seem hijacked? Sit with yourself awhile, no matter where and how you are. Consider that, instead of being overwhelmed or judging, you could simply observe your situation.

As you sit, consider that along with the challenges, other realities are also present. Consider that your troubles may have company. Love might be around somewhere. Notice in your mind someone you love. Notice someone who loves you. Sit for awhile and imagine yourself surrounded with that love.

You might feel relaxed enough now to sense some peace or contentment. Sit comfortably in your own skin. Alongside those things that stress and scare you, experience the love and peace also present. If the two eternal spiritual realities of love and peace are present, it is possible that God's grace, the source of these eternal realities, is also sitting alongside you. In fact, grace is so close to you, it is within you.

The experience will get more powerful the more often you have it. You will begin to know grace when you see it. As you dwell in it, it becomes the practice. Your consciousness of grace might come and go. It may wobble. You may distract easily. Sometimes anxiety sneaks back into the moment, and your brain is hijacked again. That's okay. Grace is only ever a thought away. When you are able, start again. Notice your physical and mental whereabouts. Remember that alongside you and your problems there is grace. Return to dwelling in it as it dwells in you. And remember to breathe.

Does Grace Think Like We Do?

Love, peace, and grace have no mind or moral conscience to screen us out or to draw us in. When we experience their lack of conditionality, we feel acceptance and intimacy with them, ourselves, and all that is around us. We just are, as grace just is. We can hardly believe such energy exists or that we have the ability to consciously experience it for a sustained amount of time. It is so contrary to our human encounters, which judge and qualify everything about us. When we let grace draw alongside, it is as though we are completely seen and known—naked and vulnerable—and still, we are loved.

If you are not sure if you believe in God, ponder for a moment, what would it be like to have unconditional love and grace attached to a being. What if that being released that energy into the universe? What if the same being made an active decision to give you these gifts?

Suddenly, grace, love, and peace are more intimate. They involve not just a spiritual reality, but an "other" distinct from us who has drawn close to us. The intentional giving of grace by God suggests that God wants to be with us, and yearns for us just as perhaps we yearn for God. Love is great, but it really comes alive when it is with another being.

What difference might the existence of a personal God who has unearned and undeserved favor for you make in how you see yourself and others? What difference would it make in your life if you companioned with grace as grace companions you? Would it change what you think about God?

Grace feels good. We feel better when we practice it daily. Life is less stressful because our minds are more open to options and to the spiritual realities we all desire. Our brains are not so often hijacked by desperate thinking. Try this practice daily and notice the difference. See if grace shifts your perspective, enlightens your mind, stirs your heart, and strengthens your will. See if it helps you love others more regularly and remain more graceful toward them more consistently.

And then there is forgiveness. See if you are able to receive or give forgiveness when grace is your companion. That is the big one. It warrants a word or ten.

"I Love You But . . ."

I knew a woman who expressed her agitation with others by saying something like, "I love you, but the way you drive gets on my nerves." It was so much a pattern that those of us who spent a lot of time with her made it into a refrain.

We all say it—if not out loud, then in our heads. While there is no limit to grace's capacity for love, forgiveness, and acceptance, humans usually think of these realities as limited commodities. We prefer to affiliate with certain people because they please us in some way. To be loved—and to love another—for love's sake alone, unearned and undeserved, this is grace. You might hear the definition of grace and think that love does the same thing. True. But love, a word that is associated with grace, is even more often described as conditional or unconditional. Love can be used to describe a feeling, a choice, an energy, a particular way of being with another person. In our thinking, we do tend to believe that love is driven by circumstances and subjectivity. "I love you but . . ." Conditional love is not bad. But when the conditions change, so does the love.

We now live in a world that encourages us to place our friends in categories (such as on Facebook). "Unfriending" is always an option and just a click away. No relationship is pleasing 100 percent of the time. Practicing grace might allow us to remain in a difficult relationship that cannot be clicked away because of life circumstances that cannot be changed. It would at least improve our personal spiritual functioning, so that we can stay present and imagine possibilities beyond the challenges. Even better, the practice of grace might ultimately transform such a relationship into something more fruitful. Grace can grow our capacity to love without the "but."

In my experience, the best place to practice grace, besides within ourselves, is in the relationships that challenge us most. Such circumstances are fertile spiritual ground. Community—wherever two or more are gathered—is a very effective place to practice grace.

Returning to one of the points of our parable, it is important to remember that grace is not fair. It is not fair when we forgive someone who has hurt us or wronged us (or we them). It is not fair when a tragedy happens on a large scale. Human beings tend to be more comfortable with the adage (which has biblical roots), "An eye for an eye, a tooth for a tooth." We want

our equal "pound of flesh" to balance the evil or the wrong committed. We want the person or people to experience the same
level of pain we feel. We perceive retribution as justice.

Think of the list of horrible people throughout history,
including those who have personally hurt you. Now brace yourself—grace is there for them too. If we earn it by good behavior,
then grace is not grace. If it really is unconditional merit and
favor, then everyone has access to it. Not everyone accepts it,
but everyone is allowed to have it. Grace is not fair. Can you live
with that?

Practicing grace, and being disciplined enough to use it as
a lens for all life, means we accept that both grace and justice
belong to God. What difference, for example, would it have made
to have forgiven Osama bin Laden after the 9/11 attacks instead
of engaging in a war that in one way or another continues more
than ten years later? Hundreds of thousands are dead, more than
were killed in the original attacks, and billions have been spent
on problems that still appear unsolvable. What might education
or health care in America look like now if we had spent that
money differently? Could we have forgiven, releasing that horrible day and all its death and destruction to the grace of God?
Instead of war could we have focused on improving our ability
to protect ourselves, strengthening our nation internally, and
moving on?

Unpopular, unthinkable, outrageous, I know. "An eye for an
eye, a tooth for a tooth" sounds like justice, but maybe letting
go would have gotten us farther as a nation. Perhaps the greater
goodness of grace would eventually have made smaller such a
grand evil.

It is an act of faith to imagine that the grace of God will
one day completely overwhelm the evil of humanity. It is an
act of faith to give up the pursuit of eyes and teeth in our own
lives, imagining more creative and effective possibilities for our
future. In the small messes of our lives and in the most hor-
rifying global atrocities, relentless pursuit of retributive justice

does not advance the cause of peace on earth. Those who pursue peace are usually the ones who end up with it.

Whether a person is willing to receive grace early in life or late, when things are going well or when life is a mess, if our conduct in life is downright evil or just a little bit bad, we still all receive the same grace. If God's goal is to share grace with humanity, then all are capable of bearing fruit and anytime is harvest time.

To those who have been practicing grace longer, there is rejoicing, not resentment. It is a blessing to witness someone light up with the freedom you feel when you know and trust you are unconditionally loved. It is a joy to walk with them as they surrender their heart, mind, and spirit into the flow of eternal life where grace holds us. The details of when and where are minor compared to such a great harvest of spiritual treasures.

Return to the Practice of Grace

Once again, practice *noticing*. Notice what you are thinking right now. As you notice where you are mentally, also notice your surroundings and where you are physically. What is consuming your mental and emotional energy today? Notice if you are linking your physical location to your thoughts and feelings. If you are sitting and reading, it might be pleasurable. On other occasions, it may be that you are thinking about something that causes you pain, and you associate it with the space you are in. Practice noticing in this physical and mental location too, with all its stress and challenge. Notice if you are able to observe the situation or if it overwhelms you.

Consider that along with the challenges other realities might also be present. Consider that grace may be with you. Ponder the notion that grace is mobile; it may go anywhere and is not confined in any way. Enhance the experience, by thinking of someone you love. Think of someone who loves you. Imagine that God loves you. Sit with that love awhile. Remember to breathe. If you are troubled by something, but also become conscious of grace, your mind will relax and some alternatives to your difficulties may begin to emerge. Explore them. Do they include grace? Love? Forgiveness? Are they spiritually elegant?

Think of someone or a situation where grace eludes you. Try to practice grace while inhabiting that thought or space. Allow grace to transform it.

Wondering Questions

What is your earliest memory of receiving grace or unearned, undeserved favor? What is your earliest memory of sharing it?

Where is it easy for you to experience grace and where is it a challenge?

Could you set aside mental and physical space each day to grow your conscious experience of God's yearning for you, rather than think about God? Could you interrupt your random thinking with the thought that grace is in you?

How do you respond when you feel someone has gotten what they did not deserve? What about when you do not get the blessings—or the punishment—you deserve?

Imagine God casting seeds of grace with abandon in the soil of your soul. Is the soil receptive? What would help make it more so? What would the harvest look like? Who can you share it with?

CHAPTER 3

Faith Is the Relationship, Commitment Is the Practice

"We started with a harvest of one bin of lettuce—400 heads—didn't we, Albert? One bin. Now it is thousands a day. Wow! And we have been figuring it out ever since."

—Bruce Taylor, CEO, to his vice president
of harvest operations, Albert Garnica,
Taylor Farms in Salinas, California

This Could Get Personal

Spirituality is personal. We tend to think of "personal" as private, solitary, silent, or isolated. Our culture has a strong message that we keep our inner life to ourselves. But by personal we might also understand we are engaged at our very core, our inmost self, the most personal, private, silent—even isolated—part of ourselves.

Spirituality is also relational. We engage with an "other," even if it is something within us we may consider off-limits from our more public self. As we engage with the unseen realities of love, peace, and grace, which are forces distinct from our being, we increase consciousness of our inner life and how our spirit works. Our encounters with this mysterious "other" make that consciousness more real, more tangible.

Acting on the belief that unseen spiritual treasures are real is called faith. Faith is where our personal spirituality and eternal, unseen realities come together and form a way of life. Or as the writer of the biblical book of Hebrews in the New Testament says it: "Now faith is the assurance of things hoped for, the conviction of things not seen" (11:1).

So far on this journey, we have been spiritually speaking about unseen but very real things: God and the gifts that come from the essence of God. You have taken a risk and trusted that by engaging the spiritual practice of *noticing* or the spiritual practice of *grace*, something will happen. Perhaps there is a shift in attitude, a little more peace, a little more love. Maybe you experienced a breakthrough in a difficult relationship because your consciousness of grace allowed you to give or receive forgiveness. Perhaps new possibilities have emerged in your life that you had not seen before. Some hope, some assurance, some *thing* keeps us going. That is faith.

You Have to Believe to See

I have faith in the spiritual teachings of Jesus. When I practice them, I experience greater spiritual awareness. My ability to apply the principles of his teachings increases fruitfulness in my life. When things do not happen on my timetable or in the form I desire, I still hope in them. I still imagine—have faith in—the possibility. I open to grace and watch for what might happen. This helps me to look for God's presence and for gifts that might come some way other than the form I first thought of them.

Talk about belief and faith usually sounds like a demand to remain on a purely intuitive, non-thinking level. In fact, inherent in spiritual practice is an intertwining of heart and mind, intellect and experience. One informs the other and we begin to know a certain spiritual logic within ourselves.

In *Christianity After Religion: The End of Church and the Birth of a New Spiritual Awakening*, Diana Butler Bass explains this well as she discusses the nature, meaning, and process of belief in Christianity. She says:

> "To believe" in Latin (the shaping language for much of Western theological thought) is *opinor, opinari*, meaning "opinion," which was not typically a religious word. Instead, Latin used *credo,* "I set my heart upon" or "I give my loyalty to," as the word to describe religious "believing," that is, "faith." In medieval English, the concept of *credo* was translated as "believe," meaning roughly the same thing as its German cousin *belieben,* "to prize, treasure, or hold dear," which comes from the root word *Liebe,* "love." Thus, in early English, to "believe" was to "belove" something or someone as an act of trust

or loyalty. Belief was not an intellectual opinion.
. . . In previous centuries, belief had nothing to
do with one's weighing evidence or intellectual
choice. Belief was not a doctrinal test. Instead,
belief was more like a marriage vow—"I do"
as a pledge of faithfulness and loving service
to and with the other. Indeed, in early English
usage, you could not hold, claim, or possess a
belief about God, but you could cherish, love,
trust in, or devote yourself to God.[13]

So the creeds or confessions of the Christian faith, or evangelical faith statements like "I accept Jesus as my Lord and Savior," may better be embraced as "I trust," or the more awkward, I "belove." I *trust* Jesus. I *belove* Jesus. I trust the faith. I belove the faith. I trust Christian community. I belove Christian community.

Jesus spoke these words. Sit with them for awhile.

With what can we compare the kingdom of
God, or what parable will we use for it? It is
like a mustard seed, which, when sown upon the
ground, is the smallest of all the seeds on earth;
yet when it is sown it grows up and becomes
the greatest of all shrubs, and puts forth large
branches, so that the birds of the air can make
nests in its shade. (Mark 4:30–32)

Mustard grows like a weed. Tiny seeds of it turn into great big trees with little effort or attention. There are many varieties. The mustard in California, seen growing like a bushy prolific sea of yellow is legendarily thought to have been cast by Spanish Roman Catholic missionary priests to mark the El Camino Real (the King's Highway). Now it is used in organic farming as a

---

13 Bass, 116–17.

cover crop to restore the soil for the next vegetable rotation. It also serves as a weed deterrent, even as it is considered a weed. Sometimes it is a nuisance, sometimes it is a blessing. Either way, it is a weed on a mission.

Jesus does not say that *we* grow like mustard plants; he says the kingdom of God grows like mustard. Elsewhere in the Gospels, Jesus says that the kingdom of God is within. When we think of the kingdom on a more personal level, maybe it equates to the spiritual realm within. Sometimes unseen spiritual realities seem so small, we think they are irrelevant. But maybe we cannot see the reality for its density. As you may have come to experience in spiritual practice, there is often more grace going on within us than we think. There is more Spirit moving inside us than we have noticed before. As with the parable of the sower, Jesus's words here imply that God is planting the kingdom on purpose. Just as mustard deters other weeds and nurtures soil, maybe within us God uses unseen spiritual realities to deter some things from growing while encouraging others.

The Power of a Strong Root System

As I walked with farmer Dirk Giannini next to what appeared to be a beautiful field of dirt, he said enthusiastically, "Do you see the new plants?" "What new plants?" I asked. "They are everywhere!" he said. As I peered closer at the dirt, I could see two tiny leaves still small as seeds themselves just emerging. One day, they would be a large leafy head of romaine lettuce.

With a more advanced plant, Dirk carefully dug the tiny seedling out of the beautiful soil to reveal a developing tap root. "Now that the seed has sprouted and started to take hold, we build the root system," he said. "If the root system is okay, then the lettuce will be robust and strong and good. We watch the plant and the soil all the time. Sometimes you starve the plant to deepen the root system, sometimes you aerate it to give it some breathing space, all for a good foundation. The art is in knowing when to do what."

We can be intentional about building our faith lives. Jesus

is the way Christians know God. Commitment to the person of Jesus and knowing more deeply the fullness of God builds a spiritual root system. Becoming an artist of our soul, as Dirk Giannini is an artist with lettuce, makes us mindful of how our personal spirituality grows. If you are not a Christian (or even if you are), could Jesus be part of your spiritual root system? Could he be the personal way you know grace and the one with whom you abide for spiritual growth?

When Jesus spoke of the kingdom of God (or the kingdom of heaven), he wanted people to take note of it, learn about it, commit to it, and grow it in the world. He invited them to participate in it and then to be like mustard seeds, spreading the kingdom everywhere. Commitment to the graceful way of Jesus is not just about the inner life, but about reflecting the values of God in the physical world.

I find Diana Butler Bass' words helpful on this point as well:

> Some may choose to participate in a certain spiritual practice because it is interesting, feels good, or gives their life new meaning, but every serious Christian practitioner soon discovers one of the deepest mysteries of these practices. Christian practices all contain within them the dimension of ethics—they all anticipate God's reign, in which the world will be made right according to God's love and justice.[14]

Nothing Is Outside the Realm of God

The world can be a crazy place. It is one of the greatest challenges to faith. We try to organize the insanity by separating good and evil, God and the Devil, justice and injustice. We may fear having faith in God because we cannot always make sense of the mysteries of life, especially tragedy, pain, and loss. But perhaps a truth of the kingdom of God is that it is capable of

---

14 Bass, 159.

holding all things together—like the complex root system of a plant, or the mustard tree in our parable—and making something good out of them. Sometimes we do not know what is good or what is evil, like whether mustard is a useful plant or a weed. Could we trust that the kingdom of God is committed to grace and justice, at the same time that it holds the very evil that seems to undermine it? Can we trust that God's graceful kingdom can hold both, and that God calls goodness forth out of what seems like confusion to us?

While on a tour of the Holy Land, I saw the cemetery next to the famed Golden Gate of the Old City of Jerusalem. This cemetery is significant for Jews, Muslims, and Christians in varying ways. People of all three traditions want to be buried there because it is considered sacred, holy ground in some way particular to their faith. As I looked out over the sea of tombstones, just over the cemetery wall, I saw a large, bushy mustard tree. It was surrounded by trash—cans, someone's leftover lunch, food wrappers, newspaper. Clearly, no one intended to plant this tree: it was too close to the wall, and there were no other trees anywhere nearby. But there it was, standing as a perfect illustration of the truth of this parable. Everything was there: new mustard seeds budding, garbage, the living and the dead, all against the backdrop of Jerusalem, itself a living metaphor for the promise and utter chaos of the world. Maybe God's realm really could hold all things.

My faith is in the power of grace to hold all things and transform all things in the end. There is a spectrum of belief around the end times (or eschatology, as scholars would call it). Some Christians believe the evil and well-behaved-but-non-believing people will go to hell, cast out of the kingdom, eternally set apart from grace. Jesus for me exhibits a much greater inclusivity than this theology allows. Paul, whose letters to Christian communities make up a large chunk of the New Testament, said nothing could ever be separated from the love of God (Romans 8:38–39) and that all creation "in heaven and on earth and under the earth" will be brought into relationship with Jesus (Philippians 2:10). I trust that this is true.

We Are in It Together

The process of faith is a relational adventure. In the beginning of a spiritual quest, we tend to be motivated by a desire to feel better and to have a stronger sense of direction for life. But as spiritual truths begin to make a positive difference, you may consider a certain commitment to the author of those truths. We can isolate the teachings of Jesus, but they are tethered to the person of Jesus. They emerge from him. For Christians, this means they come from God. Christians have faith, then, not only in the words and teachings of Jesus, which have proven true and trustworthy, but in Jesus himself. To begin to know Jesus both by reading about him and through the experience of grace is to know God.

Just as faith is relational, God is relational. Christians speak of God as "Trinity," expressed in traditional language as Father, Son, and Holy Spirit. This means God is the Father and origin of all creation; God is the Son, Jesus, who connects humanity to the fullness of God; and God is the Holy Spirit, the sustainer who offers wisdom and guidance to hold us in grace. Each one's identity and being is energized by the relationship of love and grace that the three share. One does not exist without the other. Their relationship makes them who they are distinctly, and at the same time, they are completely one.

Followers of Jesus come into relationship with this Trinity, the fullness of God, through relationship with Jesus. As the persons of the Trinity derive their identity from their relationship with one another, Christians derive our identity from life with God in Jesus Christ. As the Trinity shares divine love and grace with followers of Jesus, we go forth to share the same with the world. This is how God relates intimately within God-self and with all humanity. As I trust this relationship and the overall relationality of God, I find that my faith in God only grows.

What's in a Name?

Christians often speak of belief or faith in Jesus Christ. "Christ" is not Jesus's last name but instead a title. It refers to his calling as Messiah, the anointed one, who would be savior to the Jewish people. This concept comes with a long history, but it is enough here to say the idea that people needed a savior to save them from themselves, to overcome the grave injustices of the world and defeat evil, was fairly widespread in the first century. It still is with Jews and Christians, although we understand it in different ways. Jews await the first coming of the Messiah and believe that salvation is not for later, but something to work for now. Christians believe Jesus is the Messiah, but also work to bring about God's kingdom now and hope that Christ will come again to reorder the creation according to God's will and purpose.

Christians refer to Christ particularly when we are describing spiritual encounters with grace, which can be mystical, mysterious, or even miraculous. It is a way of highlighting the divine nature he embodies eternally. The more deeply we commit to these truths at the heart of our own lives, and seek to be rooted in his graceful way, the more we develop our "life in Christ."

Followers of Jesus who wish to experience the intimacy of this dynamic relationship and develop a conscious understanding of the Christian framework, eventually engage the spiritual practice of *commitment*.

The Spiritual Practice of Commitment

Like any practice, a spiritual practice builds our capacity for something. The spiritual practice of commitment builds our trust in Jesus's teachings, and in turn, Jesus himself. It takes us beyond intellectual belief, and into a relationship with the relational God, walking together on God's graceful way.

Allow yourself to imagine a relationship with God. Imagine that God loves you unconditionally, and imagine returning that love for God. If you do not feel it, simply pray for the capacity to love God as much as God loves you. Imagine that for today, you could commit to this relationship with the God of grace, even though life is not perfect.

When we deepen commitment, sometimes we must clean up loose ends. Do you need to forgive God for letting you down or not giving you something you asked for? Imagine forgiving God.

You may leave God tomorrow if you wish, or you may choose to continue loving God tomorrow. Sit with the possibility—the freedom—of both for a minute. Imagine loving God *today* as much as God loves you. Make it a practice that you take up one day at a time.

I Can't Believe I Am Doing This

I remember saying that to myself as I prepared to walk down the aisle at my wedding. It seemed impossible to commit for a life-time. And yet, here we are, my husband, Michael, and I, thirty years later.

It may feel odd to commit to unseen things, but it is some-thing we do throughout our lives. We commit to our families, marriages, and partnerships. We commit to friendships, jobs, physical self-care, study. We dedicate time and energy to all sorts of people and enterprises. These are seen realities, but unseen realities motivate them. I commit to my relationships because I love the people with whom I have them. I cannot literally see this love, but I know it is there. When we practice commitment, it is for the sake of that love, that bond, and the desire to deepen it.

In a marriage two people practice commitment daily. They intertwine with one another through good times and bad, highs and lows, misunderstanding and new understanding. They can have faith in the unseen gifts of God, such as love, in the midst of difficulty. Long-term couples look back and see the fruits of their practice of commitment, where at the time, they weren't sure they would make it to the next day.

A practice of commitment to a spiritual relationship with God is like that. It is an eternal union capable of surviving all circumstances of life, including physical death. Theological belief systems may shift, but faith built on loving relationship is solid. It often defies logic. After all, it does not always make logical sense for me to love my husband or for him to love me. But when he is conscious of love and I drive him crazy, he still loves me. When I am conscious of love and he drives me crazy, I still love him. In the same way, I can place my confidence in my relationship with God, even when sometimes there is no good reason to believe in God. Look at the world—there are so many reasons not to believe in God. Yet when we are conscious of God, we can believe in and commit to God. When we are conscious of the love of God, we can commit to loving God as God loves us.

As with the practices of *noticing* and *grace*, *commitment* to being conscious of the unseen love of God teaches us that when we think there is nothing there, there is more than we could have imagined. Remember the words from Hebrews: "Now faith is the assurance of things hoped for, the conviction of things not seen" (11:1). In the stories of the Gospels, those who followed Jesus sometimes did not understand where he was going or what he was doing—disciples constantly asked, "Where are you going?" "Where are we going?" "What are we doing?"—but they committed to following. Conscious of God's presence through Jesus, his followers exercised the spiritual practice of commitment to move more deeply into their life with him, even when they weren't sure about the details. And they took it one day at a time.

People struggle to believe in the resurrection of Jesus from the dead because it is physically impossible. Still, it serves as a paradigm story for Christians, not because it is provable or in need of defense, but because it speaks something of the essence of God. The resurrection reflects God's promise to keep coming back to be in relationship with humanity, even in the face of rejection. God committed to loving people one more day. This is grace: showing up against all odds, loving us when we least expect or deserve it. If we have experienced this grace, then the resurrection of Jesus might make sense. Could you have faith in God, if God has this much faith in you?

Commitment builds on the trust we develop as we grow conscious of grace. This happens little by little over the course of the relationship. It might seem a small thing. But as we have seen with the mustard seed, small things can grow very large.

Heresy Guaranteed

Some Christians are concerned about believing the right thing. We humans often want our intellectual ducks in a row. We want to organize life, even eternal life, even though that enterprise makes about as much sense as trying to nail Jell-O to a tree. God is always good for a surprise, coloring outside the lines, and jumping out of the boxes into which we have placed God.

Nonetheless, working through our language is part of making faith real. Eventually, those conversations result in something we call doctrine, or authorized statements about faith. Christians have doctrine, as do most religious groups. Our doctrine comes from the ordering of faith conversations from early Christianity. It is different than being conscious of the presence of God, but both are part of the root system of faith.

Christians engage the doctrines of our tradition as they were handed down through the years, and expressed in the earliest creeds and formulations of the faith. Those who practice commitment are bound to think about God, theology, and the world. Sometimes our conclusions will match those creeds, and sometimes they will not. If this sounds like heresy, it is. Committed Christians commit heresy regularly. We can't help it. It is part of an active spiritual life to consider and wrestle with the history, formulas, and words that shape faith.

As we have discussed, a growing proportion of Americans are "spiritual but not religious." That is, they are interested in a personal experience of spirituality and even faith, but not necessarily religious practice or doctrine. They think being religious and faithful means agreeing with all the faith statements. Some of them go to church. They may even recite the creeds, but they do not necessarily believe everything they say. They may believe

in the spiritual truth that God always comes back into relationship with humanity, but they do not buy the historical bodily resurrection of Jesus. Followers, people conscious of the *presence
of* Jesus, are not necessarily committed to the theological *statements about* Jesus.

The earliest followers of Jesus, who also lived in a period
of rapid cultural and intellectual change, had no hard and fast
creeds. They had a living experience, which grew into a growing
body of trust. They lived lives that witnessed to the power of
Jesus's life, death, resurrection, and teachings. Followers, not
doctrine, reflected faith through the spiritual practice of commitment to the graceful way of Jesus.

It is possible to substantiate this through physical evidence.
Holy sites in Israel, where Jesus is believed to have lived, taught,
been on trial, been convicted, died, and appeared in the resurrection, offer archeological evidence to support the presence not
only of Jesus, but of the generations of followers who have witnessed to his life, death, and resurrection.

But don't take their word for it. Know it for yourself through
conscious experience. We cannot believe only what others tell
us, or what ancient (and still valuable) faith formulations ask us
to recite. We must experience them as real for ourselves. For
example, I have experienced so many times the spiritual truth of
resurrection—that God keeps coming back—that the bodily resurrection of Jesus Christ himself makes sense to me.

In this postmodern world, especially given the death of institutional Christianity as it has been known for the last few hun-
dred years, we may feel we cannot trust the institution of the
church. Everyone has to reach a personal understanding of such
words as "truth," "belief," "faith," "God," "resurrection," and
more. There is much more fluidity between doctrinal adherence
and spiritual experience. This is to be expected. It is part and
parcel of life today.

Yet those who continue to follow Jesus have faith and practice commitment to walking the graceful way, trusting in the
core truths he taught and lived—one day at a time. The story

of the resurrection says Jesus was not recognizable after he rose from the dead. Long-time Christians should not, therefore, look for that which we have always seen, but for the tiny new thing taking root that may at first seem unrecognizable. Following Jesus and his graceful way, we cannot go wrong.

Return to the Spiritual Practice of Commitment

Imagine that you love God as unconditionally as God loves you. Pray that you might have the capacity to love God as God loves you. Could you forgive God for letting you down or not giving you something you asked for? Imagine that for today, you could commit to this relationship with the God of grace, even though the relationship is not perfect and neither are you. Companion with the God of grace just for today.

Wondering Questions

Could Jesus be part of your spiritual root system? Could he be the personal way you know grace and the one with whom you abide for spiritual growth?

What part of "personal relationship with Jesus" attracts you? Does anything about such a relationship seem difficult to you?

As you imagine loving God as much as God loves you, what could you do today to reflect that? What would a commitment to a life with Jesus look like? What would leaving God look like?

Where have you seen resurrection take place in your life?

CHAPTER 4

Worship Is the Genuine Response, Communion Is the Practice

"I love this dirt. Every day I pray for it and I am so happy to be here. I love laying the irrigation drip system so I can water the soil and nourish it so food for the country will grow. At the end of each day, I think, 'I have done something really good and important for our families today.'"

—Ricardo Reyes, irrigation systems,
Christensen and Giannini Farms
in Salinas, California

I Worship God on My Boat

I often hear people say they can worship anywhere, but they particularly love doing so in nature. Many people feel a stronger sense of God's presence out on the water, hiking through forests, working in the garden.

I live in a beautiful region of our country. Every day I am conscious of the intricacy of nature and that as Creator, God is reflected in all life. I, too, enjoy meditating and opening myself to God in creation. There is something effortless about engaging nature this way. It inspires wonder, imagination, silence, awe. In other words, it inspires worship, which I understand to be a genuine offering of praise, gratitude, hope, pain, or simply our very lives to God.

Many religions throughout history have organized their theology and worship around the natural order. Creation itself has been an object of worship or an icon through which people experience the creativity and order of God. It was the common human context prior to industrialization. Since the beginning of time, humans have been rejuvenated and inspired when dwelling amidst the trees, studying a seed pod, working the land, or gazing at the ocean. We can be appropriately overcome by the generative ways of creation. Indeed, research suggests that spending time in nature alters our brain chemistry in positive ways, inspiring creativity.

Several psalms captured in the Bible are creation-focused and mark the wonders of nature and the godly order of the universe. They were written for the purpose of worship, empowering a genuine response of praise to God for the beauty and fertility of the earth.

You make springs gush forth in the valleys
they flow between the hills, giving drink to every
    wild animal;
the wild asses quench their thirst.
By the streams the birds of the air have their
    habitation;
they sing among the branches.
From your lofty abode you water the mountains;
the earth is satisfied with the fruit of your work.
    (Psalm 104:10–13)

There is an understanding in these words that God has ordered the world in a particular way and all things work in concert for adequate sustenance and well-being. Harmony was instilled at the creation. The description is vibrant. Such a gift is worthy of the genuine response of praise and thanks. Could you offer a genuine response of thanks to God for something you notice in the creation today? To do so would be an act of worship, an offering of gratitude for the gifts of God.

Not just the Psalms, but several books of the Bible reflect God's ordering of the universe (and the biblical understanding is that God is the head of that order) and that we are to live respectfully within it. To live harmoniously with the creation might be considered an act of worship; that is, an outward sign of respect for the relationship we share with God.

Despite our best efforts, however, we often find ourselves in circumstances beyond our control, threatened by events rather than embraced by a perfectly functioning, benevolent universe. Storms, drought, and pestilence wreak havoc. Living gently within the created order may be a challenge, not only because we want more from it than it can give, but also because it may seem to have turned on us. When creation is out of order for our purposes, we may blame God. We may question, lose trust, and not be able to offer outward expressions of inward communion, because we do not sense it.

In the book of Job, Job—a just and faithful servant of God—loses his children, wealth, and physical well-being. He and his friends seek to work out why the creation might turn on humanity and cause suffering in the world, in particular Job's suffering. God speaks and reminds them of the enormity of creation and their humble place in it. Here are just a few of God's words to Job:

> Where were you when I laid the foundation of the earth? Tell me, if you have understanding. Who determined its measurements—surely you know! Or who stretched the line upon it? On what were its bases sunk, or who laid its cornerstone when the morning stars sang together and all the heavenly beings shouted for joy? Or who shut in the sea with doors when it burst out from the womb?—when I made the clouds its garment, and thick darkness its swaddling band, and prescribed bounds for it, and set bars and doors, and said, "Thus far shall you come, and no farther, and here shall your proud waves be stopped"? (Job 38:4–11)

There is no final answer—as far as Job knows—regarding why natural and other disasters happen. Just that, in the big scheme of things, we have our place and cannot always know about the how, what, or why of the universe. We will always have questions about suffering. God may be known in the natural order, but much mystery resides there. There will always be things in life we cannot control. All we can do, ultimately, is live with God and with each other, and keep offering both our questions and our praise to God.

All in a Day's Work

These are not the only offerings we can make to God. We can also offer our lives. When we understand our lives to be meaningful and purposeful to the wider community, we are eager to wake up every morning and get started. We are content with our place in the universe and willing to work in harmony with it. Each day is filled with a genuine response of love and gratitude for the gifts we have been given. We express this by making the most of the day ahead. We are in a way filled with a sense of humble awe for each moment of our life, not wishing to withdraw or escape, but to embrace the opportunities and challenges that lie before us. We are content to be where we are and the gestures of our lives reflect that. In short, we could use words such as gratitude, communion, humility, praise, awe, and self-offering to help us understand what it means to worship.

Ricardo, quoted in the beginning of this chapter, has worked on the same farm for twenty-four years. He loves his life's work. When he speaks of it, there is a sense of being connected to God, the earth, and other human beings. Laying irrigation seems a spiritual experience for Ricardo. He does not take for granted the greater purpose of his work. He reflects on it quite deeply, which generates in him a sense of personal well-being, self-worth, and devotion to the earth. It seems every day is one of spiritual generativity for Ricardo.

Others do not find such contentment in their day-to-day life. They close down their creativity instead of being open to it. Novelist Barbara Kingsolver wrote *Animal, Vegetable, Miracle* as an account of her family's effort to eat only food grown in their county for a solid year. Their goal was to live within the created order as it was given, rather than manipulating it to their liking.

The problem was they still wanted to find meat sources for protein, so they resolved to breed their own turkeys. They had to learn the way most turkeys come to our dinner tables, and the news was not good. Because the goal is to breed as many turkeys as possible, the system does not rely on the turkeys doing what comes naturally. Instead, she discovered this:

> The sperm must be artificially extracted from
> live male turkeys by a person, a professional
> turkey sperm-wrangler if you will, and artifi-
> cially introduced to the hens, and this is all I am

going to say about that. If you think they send the toms off to the men's room with little paper cups and *Playhen* Magazine, that's not how it goes. I will add only this: if you are the sort of parent who threatens your teenagers with a future of unsavory jobs when they ditch school, here's one more career you might want to add to the list.[15]

How excited would you be to get up every day and do this work? You might approach it as Ricardo did, or being the professional turkey sperm-wrangler might take a toll on your spirit and on your creativity. I hesitate to include such an example, but as we know, life is not always bucolic in the agricultural world. There are dirty, seedy, smelly, spirit-depleting, low-quality, cost-efficient, and unjust means by which our food gets to the table each day. And there are many similarly unsatisfying places—some of which require a business suit but are nonetheless spirit depleting—where people must spend their days.

Such environments can wear on a person over time. Quite possibly, you might begin to mirror the physical infertility of the turkeys with your own spiritual infertility, convinced this is all there is to life. Such a spiritual posture is contrary to God's desire for our lives to be creative and generative, and to offer those fruits as our worship.

When I do not like what I am doing, I can feel held hostage by life. I may close down into resentment instead of opening up into wonder. I can render myself spiritually infertile. While our circumstances do not have the power to cause our thoughts and feelings, sometimes we think they do. Sometimes people allow one thought to govern their whole lives. In turn, they lose the ability to imagine something beyond where they are. We can't

15 Barbara Kingsolver, Stephen Hopp, and Camille Kingsolver, *Animal, Vegetable, Miracle: A Year of Food Life* (New York: Harper-Collins, 2007), 90.

possibly consider change and cannot be truly worshipful if we believe we are stuck and that our circumstances dictate our lives. They do not. Circumstances do not cause us to feel anything. Our thinking about those circumstances is what generates our feelings. How we think determines if we feel hopeful, loved, happy, peaceful, content, trapped, resentful, angry, hurt, or discontent. When we think differently about a person or a situation, we can change our feelings. We may not always be able to stop thinking, but we always have a choice about what to think. Such a discipline gives us freedom, self-control, empowerment, fertility. It makes life more worshipful.

To Whom All Hearts Are Open

Worship is a genuine response to God, life, ourselves. When we open ourselves in wonder, praise, and humble presence in the creation, when we lament in the tragedies and grief of life, when we are enlightened to greater creativity, and when we experience deep communion with God, we are worshipping. We are laying it out there, telling the truth about how and why we think and feel the way we do. Worship is honesty.

It is a mistake to think that worship should only occur when we feel good, such as when walking in the woods or gazing at the ocean. Or when we are in a particular place, such as a gorgeous Gothic church with stained-glass windows and vaulted ceilings. Worship is a holistic experience that involves every bit of us and every bit of God, known and unknown. It is not confined to a happy mood or a suitable location.

When we open ourselves to God's presence, we trust that God can cope with our thoughts, feelings, and circumstances, no matter what they are. We have faith in God. We lift our hearts and minds beyond ourselves, trusting we are not bound by our feelings. In this inner gesture, we are choosing the path of grace, releasing the disempowering thought that circumstances control the fruitfulness of our lives.

If what we want from God is a guarantee that life will always be blissful, we will forever be disappointed. God's grace is not an inoculation against events. The Christian life promotes spiritual living that helps us move gracefully and steadily through the storms of life as they come and go. It is not a shield against those challenges. The offering of our genuine response to God is a reciprocal gesture toward God, who has been present and honest with us in Jesus.

In Jesus's life, likewise, there is a genuine response to God that takes in the fullness of human experience, joy, healing, and empowerment, but also abandonment and suffering. In Matthew's version of Jesus's story, when Jesus dies, he believes he has been forsaken on the cross by God. Jesus cries out, "My God, my God, why have you forsaken me?" (Matthew 27:46). Who wouldn't ask that question? It is an honest and open gesture challenging God to be present to Jesus's agony. To express one's experience of separation from God or at least the silence of God—this is also an honest act of worship. If Jesus—who was both fully human and fully God—could make this genuine expression, can you trust God enough to say what is real for you?

Some churches begin worship with a prayer written in the sixteenth century by Thomas Cranmer called the Collect for Purity. It sums up this radically open posture beautifully.

> Almighty God, to you all hearts are open, all desires known, and from you no secrets are hid: Cleanse the thoughts of our hearts by the inspiration of your Holy Spirit, that we may perfectly love you, and worthily magnify your holy Name, through Jesus Christ our Lord. Amen.[16]

In worship, you are welcome to sit gently with your truth and with God. Try it now.

---

16 The Book of Common Prayer (New York: Church Publishing, 1979), 355.

Jesus spoke these words. Sit with them for awhile.

> Jesus said, "What do you think? A man had two sons; he went to the first and said, 'Son, go and work in the vineyard today.' He answered, 'I will not,' but later he changed his mind and went. The father went to the second and said the same; and he answered, 'I go, sir,' but he did not go. Which of the two did the will of his father?"
>
> They said, "The first." Jesus said to them, "Truly I tell you, the tax collectors and the prostitutes are going into the kingdom of God ahead of you. For John came to you in the way of righteousness and you did not believe him, but the tax collectors and the prostitutes believed him; and even after you saw it, you did not change your minds and believe him." (Matthew 21:28–32)

This parable is part of a group of four (including the parable of the laborers we explored in chapter 2) that come just after Jesus enters the city of Jerusalem, where he will be put to death. They are often thought of as "judgment parables." Contextually, they were directed toward those who accepted Jesus and those who did not. The parable suggests that it is the orientation of our hearts and minds that convicts us, rather than the weight of the moral wrongs we have committed. John, a prophet who happened to be Jesus's cousin, called people to repentance; that is, he made space for people to speak honestly about their lives. Jesus is saying that to repent, speak honestly, and change one's mind, even after a lifetime of immoral living, is better than to keep lying about your truth.

In first-century Palestine, farms and vineyards were family affairs. Everyone in a family had a role to play and work to do. At a young age females were married out of their family of origin and sent with a dowry, part of the social and economic interplay of family systems that supported day-to-day survival. Patrilineal inheritance was the norm, with the eldest son inheriting the largest amount of property from the father. As the eldest, he began work sooner than his siblings, all boys starting more serious work around age fourteen. Subsequent sons, inheriting less, would still remain close to home. Social mobility in any direction was limited. Where would the brothers in this parable go if they chose not to work in their father's vineyard? This was their inheritance, their lot in life. That they might have tried to avoid their responsibility is an interesting notion in and of itself. Perhaps they felt like a turkey sperm-wrangler might have and, if only for a day, wanted to avoid their reality altogether.

In this parable, no one changes their occupation or station in life in order to receive God's favor. Their circumstances do not appear to change at all, as far as we can tell. The sons are sons, the tax collectors and prostitutes are tax collectors and prostitutes. They are all referred to in the present tense. What is different is that some have an honest posture with God. They eagerly open themselves, sin and all, desirous for God's presence and God's graceful way. They seek the reordering of life that God's grace offers. They choose to receive it and, in their self-offering of honesty and transformation, they worship God with their whole being.

The Spiritual Practice of Communion

The spiritual practice of *communion,* then, is to live as much as possible a sustained experience of God's presence over time. As we do this, we live worshipful lives, and soon our inner life of communion flows into our day-to-day living. In this practice, you can become mindful of your thoughts, disciplining yourself to return to grace when you have left it.

One way to do this is to practice noticing when you are caught in the idea that circumstances cause feelings, or when you have gotten in the habit of blaming others for how you feel or what you are experiencing. Remember a time when you were angry or resentful toward someone else. You may be able to recollect that sometimes the feelings were more intense than at other times. Sometimes you were really angry, sometimes a little angry, and sometimes you could think of that person or situation and not be angry at all. The feelings changed, but the circumstances did not. If circumstances caused our feelings, then this would not be the case.

Ponder for a moment that the way you were thinking about the person or the event in a given moment made a difference in how you were feeling. Consider that a thought is just a thought and a feeling is just a feeling.

Then think for a moment on grace. Remember God's unconditional love and desire for you. Imagine grace companioning you, dwelling within you. Notice the difference in your thinking even after just a minute. Remaining conscious of the presence of grace in your mind could create in you deep peace, no matter what is happening in your life. It could open you to new possibilities and empower you to change things that previously seemed to hold you hostage. You could become more spiritually fertile. You might even embrace laying irrigation or turkey sperm-wrangling for a living. Understood in this way, even our thoughts are a gesture of worship, a practice of communion with God.

Will yourself to trust God even when you would rather trust your own emotions. Notice when your day-to-day living drifts away from communion with God. Living this rational process of recognizing the relationship between our thoughts and our spiritual generativity is critical to a centered, peaceful, and spiritually elegant life.

The practice of communion is both a personal one and a corporate one. We are in communion with God while in solitude, and also with others in community. Both are beneficial and good for growing a life of grace. For Christians, we understand grace to be the way of Jesus and we seek to follow it. The practice of communion helps us to live this with intention.

This Is Where Other People Come In

We have so far spoken of worship in individual ways. You lift a joyful heart in adoration, praise, and thanksgiving for God's gifts. You honestly speak your experience to God. You risk trust, opening yourself to a reordering of your life through that honesty. But in most religions worship is also corporate. Many of the psalms, for example, were used in gathered worship rather than for individual devotion or prayer. All religions meet as a body, usually moving through rituals of prayer, acknowledging God's holiness, listening to sacred writings, and, in the case of some Christians, celebrating the sacraments.[17] These of course take various forms and styles. At its heart, though, corporate worship is the opportunity, the spiritual practice, of communing with God and other people at the same time. The synergism of a group can be very powerful.

In the early days of the Christian faith, worship happened in house churches or other more private venues. Early followers of Jesus were controversial and unpopular with the established religions of the day. Worship was sometimes in secret, with strict boundaries for membership. Corporate worship began to take on shape and form based on the tradition, teaching, and contextual experience of people living their faith. Worship was designed for communion with God, for building up the body of those already following Jesus's way of grace, but also to draw new members into the community by teaching them to live this way too.

As today, congregations of the early church would have prayed and sang together, studied the scriptures, and shared what we would now call Holy Eucharist or Communion. Very generally speaking, while now we see a great diversity in worship, from a focus on the teaching in evangelical churches, to very formal, more orchestrated worship, this breadth did not come

---

17 The two primary sacraments in Christianity are baptism and Eucharist, or Holy Communion. The word sacrament is traditionally understood as an "outward and visible sign of an inward and spiritual grace." The Book of Common Prayer, 857.

about until the Reformation. In the early years as Christianity became an institution in addition to a living faith, its form of worship would have been more uniformly sacramental, that is Eucharistic. The worshipful act of Communion itself was the spiritual practice exercised by a body of believers in one place.

When the Reformation occurred, many new forms of worship emerged out of shifts in theology and views about how church should be organized and expressed. Political nationalism had a lot to do with this, as Christianity took root in its local context. In all churches though, now as then, Christians will follow a rhythm of worship patterned on the life, death, and resurrection of Jesus. For Christians, we engage the fullness of Jesus's life so we may learn to live ours in the same graceful way. We help each other do this when we worship together.

Christmas (the birth of Christ) and Easter (the resurrection of Christ) are the primary events of Jesus's life around which churches orient their worship life. More evangelical churches celebrate less dramatically (if at all) the ancient festivals, holy days, and saints days that more catholic, historic, sacramental churches embrace. In addition, patterns of reading the scriptures will vary, with some pastors of congregations personally selecting readings on which to preach. Other churches organize readings using a cyclic calendar called a lectionary.

For many Christians, Eucharist, which literally means thanksgiving, is an important spiritual practice of communion, both the spiritual and the physical kind. For some churches, Eucharist takes the shape of a memorial of what Jesus did at his Last Supper with his friends before he died (Matthew 26:17–30 or Luke 22:7–23). For some it is a ritual of spiritual and mystical union, in which we are joining with the eternal presence of Jesus and becoming one with him. No matter the theology or religious tradition, Holy Eucharist is an outward gesture that nurtures our inner life and our communal life with God and other Christians.

No matter the style, good worship or liturgy has a sense of flow that carries the worshipper into a spiritual encounter with the living God. There is an authentic offering of those gathered, and even when all the participants do not fully understand what is happening, they have an experience of God's mystery, holiness, and inclusion through word, song, prayer, gesture, mood, and space. In worship people can discover the deep communion between God and humanity that Christians know through the life, death, and resurrection of Jesus. When we gather as a group in the consciousness of that sacred story, we often have an exponential experience of grace.

The culture of any church can be daunting and confusing for the uninitiated. The Christian journey will eventually involve learning something of history, and understanding that which is spiritually edifying and theologically formative to those gathered in a particular congregation. Even within the same denomination or tradition, there can be a great variety of worship styles and emphases. If you are looking for a church in which to worship, experiencing the personality and spiritual character of a congregation will be important. Do you resonate with the people, the community, the style and content of worship? They are not all the same. Who you are will make a difference in the sort of church you might call home.

Some people may wonder why any of us take the time to go to church each week. Why not have your individual spiritual journey? Communal worship offers the opportunity to join with other followers of Jesus and reorient your heart and mind to the way of grace. For Christians, it is a primary medium for communicating that God is present, loves all people, and has given us the fullness of life through Jesus. We sing it, say it, pray it, and gesture it. We seek to embody it as best we can. We wish to invite others into a faith where lives are transformed. In other words, beautiful worship inspires our spiritual fertility and makes us ready for a creative week. For some of us, it is as wondrous as gazing at the ocean or walking in the forest.

While I can worship in solitude on a boat, or in private reflection, the mix of a human gathering produces something different than individual meditation. Suddenly, you have to deal with the reality of other people. Corporate worship more properly mirrors real life, and there is, in my experience, a greater chance of spiritual fertility when there are other people around. Worship like this can carry an already content person to greater contentment and inspire that person to share it in some way with others. It can assure a person who is struggling that they are not alone, especially because another person who could help might literally be in the room with them. It can lift your soul when you cannot lift it yourself. It can call you to openness with God. It can help you to forgive and move toward greater freedom. As grace is available to each of us individually, it also pours out on us as a body.

Return to the Spiritual Practice of Communion

The spiritual practice of *communion,* then, is to live as much as possible a sustained experience of God's presence and grace over time. It is connecting our whole lives to God through increased mindfulness of what we are thinking, returning to the thought of grace whenever we leave it.

Practice noticing when you are caught in the idea that circumstances cause feelings, or when you find yourself in the habit of blaming others for your state. Seek to trust grace even when you would rather trust your own perceptions and power. Imagine that God dwells with you, that God's grace makes a difference, especially in the parts of your life that feel out of your control. Invite God to be present in these places, or carry them to God. When you do this, you are actively engaged in communion.

The spiritual practice of communion necessarily involves others. We practice not only within ourselves, but with other people. Remain open to finding a worshipping community where you might be spiritually at home. If you already have one, open more deeply to true communion with God and the people around you.

Wondering Questions

When have you had an experience of worship? Inside a church? Outside of a church? What was it like for you?

How would you describe "communion" with God?

What sorts of gestures in organized worship draw you and make you want to join them? What touches your soul?

What are outer signs in your day-to-day life of your inner communion with God?

What painful or frustrating circumstances tend to shut you down? Which ones would you have the hardest time sharing with God? Try sharing these with God, and over time notice whether your feelings about those circumstances begin to change.

CHAPTER 5

Community Is the Way, Relationships Are the Practice

"They say once you work in produce, versus other food sectors, you never leave. I have worked for Coca-Cola and another large corporate firm. Aside from the size of those operations, there is just something about bringing food out of the dirt that is so amazing and so real. . . . Every day is a challenge, interesting, exciting, miraculous really. The science of it, every pathogen, every organism, everything is a part of the whole."

—Tanya Mason, vice president of
business development, Taylor Farms

I Need My Space

The natural order of the creation is one of great intimacy. Perhaps we are in such awe of nature because we see how perfectly *absolutely everything* works together. Maybe we also want to feel that connected, that close, to our life's work, to our families and our friends, to God. Perhaps we would enjoy in our own lives the same synergism and balance we see in nature. Yet, as products of our Western culture, we may be reluctant to give up our self-definition, our self-determined space. We may not be sure we want the commitment, self-giving, and accountability that is involved in such a common life.

I think of a young woman known to a friend of mine who committed suicide because she had only twenty-five Facebook friends. She may have been caught in deep depression, but no one around her knew. How sad that she was not sufficiently connected to herself, friends, or family to have the value of her life affirmed. How sad she had no words to cry out that may have directed her longing toward something beyond herself. The poetic words of Psalm 63 express just such a longing. "O God, you are my God, I seek you, my soul thirsts for you: my flesh faints for you, as in a dry and weary land where there is no water." The writer, perhaps wandering in the desert, is exhausted and deeply desires the companionship of God—or anyone. In our highly individual culture sometimes we wander in a spiritual desert. As one preacher I heard recently pointed out, "When we use the word 'longing,' it is usually about a car." Material things do not satisfy the deep need of the soul for community.

Is it possible that at the heart of all longing, there is a desire to be in communion with God and with one another? Are we willing to give up even a small amount of self-determination to be in community?

In the Judeo-Christian tradition, in the stories of the Bible on which we meditate, it is clear that community and being connected to others is part of God's ordering of the human life. The message is clear from the first creation stories in the book of Genesis; people are meant to partner with one another and with the creation. In the New Testament, the early churches are strongly encouraged to care for their unity while working through their theological and relational differences. And all the craziness of life is in each community—just like any dysfunctional family! You can see interdependence, relationship challenges, and synergistic creativity in all the parables we have read: seeds and soil, laborers and harvest, small things growing large, family dynamics, and personal sinfulness and dysfunction all mixed up with the wider community. These stories and teachings are both real and a metaphor for how all of life works. Nothing is truly isolated from anything else. We cannot survive without one another for long, even if we do sometimes drive each other crazy.

I travel regularly in Western Tanzania to visit churches there. It is a highly communal culture. My Tanzanian friends do not understand our individualism; meanwhile, Westerners can find being with people, reliant on them all the time, quite tiring. A friend said one day, "I would find it so strange if each morning I did not greet all of my neighbors." She intentionally leaves her home and greets her immediate neighbors each and every day. One assumes the neighbors do the same.

Another African friend, a Ugandan immigrant to the United States and a Roman Catholic priest, knocked on the apartment door of the parish's head pastor every morning to greet him. After about six weeks, the pastor, a European, asked, "Why do you bother me every single morning?" My friend understood his cultural misstep with his pastor over time, but he said it took him two years to be comfortable with not engaging his pastor and others he passed each morning.

Meanwhile, in America, our culture continues its march toward extreme individualism. Growing up in the southeastern United States where people regularly "dropped by for a visit," I was accustomed to my mother keeping the front rooms of the house in order just in case. Often people did visit, and we stopped what we were doing and sat on the front porch or in the living room and chatted for awhile. Living in California, my family rolls their eyes at me when I say we need to keep things picked up, just in case. People in this region do not stop by unannounced; it would be too much a violation of personal space.

As our culture values mobility, personal control, and independence more and more, we continue to compartmentalize life to the point where we do not know our neighbors and the challenges of our own communities, or necessarily even care about them. We struggle to understand the complexity of world politics or economics and participate responsibly. And, of course, pointing to one of the themes of this book, we are even disconnected from how our food, our most basic sustenance, is grown. Roughly a third of our children do not know where milk, bacon, or butter comes from, let alone can they identify the most basic vegetables and fruits. Ten percent of American healthcare costs are food related, a number that will double in ten years.[18] Remaining disconnected from the basic relational aspects of life, of which food and people are two, may well be killing us. There is only so much our bodies and spirits can take.

Christianity Is Not for Loners

Christianity is inherently relational. As previously noted, the doctrine of the Trinity is grounded in community. Craig Van Gelder and Dwight Zscheile, authors of *The Missional Church in Perspective,* summarize it in this way:

> The Trinity is seen as a community whose orientation is outward, and whose shared love

---

18 http://www.jamieoliver.com/us/foundation

spills over beyond itself. Moreover, the concept of *perichoresis*, or the mutual indwelling/inter-penetration of the three persons in a dynamic, and circulating movement, has offered rich analogies for human interdependence and relational community. In this Trinitarian perspective, to be a person is to participate in others' lives, to have an identity shaped by other persons, rather than to be an isolated individual.[19]

This is pretty technical language, but the point is that I can be myself, even as I know my identity derives from relationship with others. Christians understand that we are made by and for relationships. We are made in the image of God, who is a relational being. We are drawn into the communion of God— the traditional language being "Father, Son, and Holy Spirit"— through our relationship with Jesus Christ. When we are part of the church, the community of God, we reflect this into the world, inviting others to join us. The relationship that *is* God gives birth to our personal relationship *with* God, and in turn the relationship that is the body of Christ, the church, is created.

Some days are better than others at church. As with any human institution, churches can be routine, mundane, and uninspiring. Worse, the walls of churches can hide sexual abuse, financial misconduct, emotional and spiritual manipulation, and various other human failings. I do not blame people for looking at the church overall and not wanting to be part of it. As some of us say in jest but also sincerity: "We are full of self-righteous sinners—and there is always room for one more." Christianity is a living faith and as such it deals with real life. Church can create community and tear it apart, because, while God is in it, so are people. And things are sure to get messy when people are involved.

The church above any other institution should be ever

19 Craig Van Gelder and Dwight Zscheile, *The Missional Church in Perspective* (Grand Rapids, MI.: Baker Books, 2011), 105.

thankful for grace. As people who have committed to sharing grace in the world, we are in particular need of it ourselves. As with any individual, there is always another opportunity for the church to live more gracefully.

Genuinely responding to God, practicing spiritual communion, trusting God enough to tell the truth of our reality, and rediscovering God's order for our lives are all part of the Christian life. The church as an intentional and committed gathering of individual followers of Jesus must do the same as a collective body. When an institution is honest about itself, even allowing parts of itself to pass away, it witnesses to the graceful way of Jesus: that through living his story of life, death, and resurrection, we discover new life yet again.

There is no single way to be church. The Holy Spirit, present at the birth of the church, is wildly diverse but eternally rooted in the relationship that is God. Christians understand that the Holy Spirit is the guiding presence of God, the one who offers on-the-spot wisdom and instruction for all things personal and communal. For those of us who are in the community of the church, we ask the Holy Spirit to teach and guide us about how to be a body of followers faithful to Jesus and the values we experience in his graceful way. We ought to invite the Spirit to correct us, give us courage to try new things, strengthen us, energize us, and inspire us.

While churches differ on how Christian community is organized, we agree that in a mystical and mysterious way we are one in Christ, a unified body all connected through the one we follow. We express this understanding by elevating relationships to a very high status. We believe they reflect what God values: unity, interdependence, and the untold fruits of staying in relationship in order to learn how to be reconciled to one another. This is sometimes challenging spiritual work.

Two of the most famous things Jesus said are, "Love one another as I have loved you" (John 15:12) and "Love your neighbor as yourself" (Mark 12:31). They are slightly different, but both suggest that we engage the discipline not of merely liking someone, but loving them at least as well as you love your-self. The book of Leviticus in the Hebrew Bible contains myriad religious, moral, and ethical codes, but these same laws trans-late best in very concrete ways, such as "cherish the stranger," meaning take care of them as you would something beloved. Willing ourselves to love friend, foe, or stranger is one of the ways we strengthen our unity. Christians should be less con-cerned with agreement on how we think about God and instead dwell in the love of God.

Jesus spoke these words. Sit with them for awhile.

> I am the true vine, and my Father is the vine-grower. He removes every branch in me that bears no fruit. Every branch that bears fruit he prunes to make it bear more fruit. You have already been cleansed by the word that I have spoken to you. Abide in me as I abide in you. Just as the branch cannot bear fruit by itself unless it abides in the vine, neither can you unless you abide in me. I am the vine, you are the branches. Those who abide in me and I in them bear much fruit, because apart from me you can do nothing. Whoever does not abide in me is thrown away like a branch and withers; such branches are gathered, thrown into the fire, and burned.
>
> If you abide in me, and my words abide in you, ask for whatever you wish, and it will be done for you. My Father is glorified by this, that you bear much fruit and become my disciples.
>
> As the Father has loved me, so I have loved you; abide in my love. If you keep my com-mandments, you will abide in my love, just as I have kept my Father's commandments and abide in his love. I have said these things to you so

that my joy may be in you, and that your joy
may be complete.

This is my commandment, that you love one
another as I have loved you. No one has greater
love than this, to lay down one's life for one's
friends. You are my friends if you do what I
command you. I do not call you servants any
longer, because the servant does not know what
the master is doing; but I have called you friends,
because I have made known to you everything
that I have heard from my Father. You did not
choose me but I chose you. And I appointed you
to go and bear fruit, fruit that will last, so that
the Father will give you whatever you ask him
in my name. I am giving you these commands
so that you may love one another. (John 15:1–17)

Jesus's words, a metaphor more than a parable, reflect the
connection of his followers to him, the followers to one another,
and Jesus to the Father. The words can feel confusing because
they reflect such overlapping relational intimacy. The Spirit
makes an entrance a little later in the gospel, but we can assume
its presence here too, since all the other players of the community of God are included.

The word "abiding" suggests the same concept as "communion." There is a relational union that bears fruit, a life of complete joy, service, mutuality, and friendship. What a beautiful
description of Christian community Jesus gives his followers.
Every church should aspire to this relational life of abiding in
God, God abiding in us, our mutual abiding in one another.

The instructions to live as a healthy vine are quite clear: love
as you have been loved by Jesus, that is, by grace. Serve one
another from that same love, and bear fruit in your personal life,
in the community, and the wider world. Imagine your life with
God and others as a vine. Is that a helpful image for you?

Then There Is the Pruning

Pruning can sound painful and scary, recalling experiences of rejection and isolation. I do not think Jesus has in mind that a person is pruned out of a community, but rather that we all need spiritual pruning, individuals and communities alike. He even says the Father prunes him. This is part of spiritual growth of being who God wants us to be. As followers of Jesus, can we trust God to prune us in grace?

Carey Ellen Walsh in *The Fruit of the Vine: Viticulture in Ancient Israel* notes the following:

> Pruning requires some management decisions for the next year's harvest. That is, if the vintner decides to prune lightly to reap an abundant crop one year, the fruitfulness of his buds for the following year diminishes. An unpruned vine will have from 10 to 100 times the buds necessary for a good crop of quality grapes. The vintner, then, must exercise a certain amount of discipline for the sake of longer-term goals. . . . Conservative pruning enhances stability in production from year to year and so makes the most sense as a long-term strategy for the ancient vintner. While a one-time big harvest would have delighted the first-time vintner, he would probably not repeat the mistake in subsequent years.[20]

The growing conditions of a vineyard do not do all the work. It is not just about the soil, the seeds, or the birds. Harvest does not randomly occur. Pruning is an art, it involves strategy, and it is essential to a healthy vine and its branches. Proper pruning assures long-term, stable growth. Vintners and pruners work closely together to understand all the factors at work on the vines and the branches and where exactly to make the cut. The most

---

20 Carey Ellen Walsh, *The Fruit of the Vine: Viticulture in Ancient Israel* (Winona Lake, ID.: Eisenbrauns, 2000), 119–20.

artful and knowledgeable pruners will sometimes be employed
by vineyards year-round, doing other tasks, so they are available
for those few weeks a year when pruning the vines is required.
It is that important.

Pruning causes stress in the vine, but only the good kind
of stress. To trim one shoot frees nutrition and energy to flow
into another part of the vine. Fruit, therefore, is "forced" out in
a particular direction by pruning. Managing conditions through
pruning will make the vine more fruitful. If you leave a vine
unpruned, you may get one good harvest, but in subsequent
years, you will just get leaves. Leaves make bad wine.

The other fact about pruning is that a vine cannot do it
for itself. It needs an "other" to do the pruning. When we read
about the vine and the branches, we can see the metaphor for
our personal spiritual lives, but also for the church. We can see
the Spirit as one who prunes us through wisdom and instruction. We can understand that through our personal communion
with God, extreme individualism and isolation are challenged
by the pruning action of overwhelming love. We can see how
the worship, teaching, fellowship, and justice work of a spiritual
community could change us, make us more fruitful. Just being
exposed to the needs of others in any kind of community can
prune away our own selfishness.

God wants the church around for awhile. It is intended to
bear the fruit of grace. The only way that works is if everyone
who is part of a church community is open to being pruned on
a regular basis for God's long-term strategy. Just as individuals
reflect spiritual elegance when they develop their spirituality
over a lifetime, a church can reflect such depth when it opens to
the changes called forth by the Spirit.

All this pruning is not done by one who is uncaring or unre-
lated, sweeping in to trim but otherwise absent. In the Gospel of
John (which is quite different than Matthew, Mark, and Luke),
Jesus refers to his followers as his friends, expressing a relational
equality and unity that encompasses all the ups and downs of
real life. Friends are not separate from the communion of God or

subservient to it in a hierarchical way; rather, they are relationally fully part of it. As Jesus derives identity from the Father, so the friends derive their sense of self from Jesus. The Spirit holds and keeps the friends in communion one with another. Through abiding, or indwelling in Christ, we are one. Not all the same, but one. The friends of Jesus are willing to be accountable in such a way that life will be fruitful for the glory of God. Followers of Jesus, then, give up elements of their self-determination and receive pruning in order to live as God would like them to live.

The Spiritual Practice of Relationship

Some relationships are easy, some are challenging, but they all require attention. They can all benefit from the spiritual practices outlined in the previous chapters. Relationships as spiritual practice deploy all the other practices of noticing, grace, commitment, and communion. To be in relationship with another means we must notice them, gracefully love, accept, and commit to them, and experience communion with them. We may need to set boundaries, but we do not wander off when life with another gets hard. We do not ignore strangers, especially ones in need.

In this spiritual practice we begin by acknowledging the humanity of another. This sounds easier than it is. We are often unaware of the stereotypes, prejudices, and judgments that we use to categorize people. It may be efficient to group our thoughts and perceptions about people, but it is not the way of love.

As part of this practice, notice people as you pass them on the street. Greet your coworkers, the homeless person on the corner, the irate driver in the other car—reverence their reality in some way. Be creative in the practice as you find ways to do this that place people at ease. Discover ways of being in graceful communion with another, if just for a moment. Even a few seconds of loving kindness can make a difference for a person who feels unnoticed in life. Most people will not bite or stalk you if you give them a little attention.

Small doses of attentive love help us to see the power of the practice of relationship. They build our confidence and spiritual stamina for longer-term relationships of unconditional love. As you enter that generally more challenging level of relationship, love that person minute by minute instead of year by year. Commit to the relationship sixty seconds at a time. If you fail in one minute, another one will be right behind it. You can try to be more graceful in that next minute. You will have 1,440 chances each and every day. At some point you will make progress.

I remember seeing the spiritual practice of relationship in action when my daughter was six years old. We had just moved to Miami from California. She entered a new school and promptly got sick with more than a run-of-the-mill cold. She needed a doctor. We did not yet have our own, so we took a referral.

We waited for ninety minutes before getting into the examining room. In California, two o'clock means two o'clock, so I was not used to the flexible understanding of the word "appointment" in Miami. I was sure the doctor would be a flake. Dr. Rives entered the examining room—all four feet and eleven inches of her. I further dehumanized her for her short stature.

I had low expectations, so I was taken aback when Dr. Rives got my limp child onto the examining table, looked into her sullen eyes, and said, "So how are you, Katie?" just as present and kind as Jesus himself.

Her attentiveness freed my mind. Katie sniffled and began to cry and pour out her heart to Dr. Elvira Rives, who listened as this child disclosed the woes of a new house, and new friends, and now a very bad sore throat. Dr. Rives listened to her, not once losing eye contact. When she began to examine her, Dr. Rives talked about when she was close to Katie's age. She had left her parents and her country and come to America from Cuba, living with an aunt, speaking no English. Together they talked about how hard it was to move to a new place and begin again. Despite the differences between their experiences, their reverence for one another was a beautiful thing to behold. My mind was reordered to a more loving and graceful state, watching the practice of relationship.

It turned out Dr. Rives was a committed Christian. When I am having a bad relationship day, I think of her workload serving so many children and families both in her office and in the hospital. I am inspired by her stamina and her ability to commit to the practice of relational attentiveness.

Practicing at the Advanced Level

There is also what I call the advanced spiritual practice of relationships. This is when we work on relationships that have been overwhelmed by brokenness, division, hurt, and defensiveness. These require patience, rebuilding trust, and sheer will. This does not typically happen overnight but over months or years. In our materialistic and individualistic culture, this does not come easily to us. Grace is only ever a thought away, but sometimes it takes awhile to have the thought.

The spiritual practice of communion, that is, the sustained experience of grace, is key in the advanced practice of relationships. The discipline of this practice is bringing our mind home to grace until it is rewoven into the fabric of the relationship. It requires keen awareness of our thinking as we move through times of relational challenge. Those of us who live in cultures that value individuality and personal space may resist this. When someone hurts me, it means they have invaded my personal space; they have encroached on my will and my right to manage all my experiences. They hurt me without my permission. It may seem sensible to carve a moat around my emotional castle at that point, in order to prevent further incursion.

Forgiveness is part of relational living. It is what God does with us and we do with God. It is a vital practice we can take up with one another. Forgiveness on the part of the one harmed, and conscious humility and change on the part of the offender, are reciprocal spiritual gestures that over time open us to the healing of a broken relationship. In some chronic cases, it may need to be a lifetime practice. There may be instances where physical separation is necessary or where not all those in the relationship want to forgive, be forgiven, or change. One can always practice forgiveness even if others do not share in that work. It will be as transforming as we allow it to be.

Prayer as Relationship

In the previous chapter, I mentioned prayer briefly as part of worship. In worship settings, this generally refers to corporate prayer for the concerns of the worshipping body, its community, the church, and the world. Sharing prayer in this way is a relational practice, but so is prayer one-on-one or in small groups. In spiritual communities such as the church, people pray for one another. We are literally together, sometimes sitting quietly, but often listening to the concerns of another and helping to bear them. Few things are more intimate than having another person pray for something that is a worry to us or offer praise when our hearts are full of joy. Prayer for one another builds the unity of a church, of a friendship, and of a family.

I visited with a colleague in the church recently whom I had not seen in a year and whom I do not see often. Within a few minutes of speaking, she asked about a particular concern I shared before and for which she had committed to pray. That she asked so promptly suggested to me she had been disciplined in prayer for me for the entire year. How great is that?

Prayer is an outward gesture of care that reflects an internal, graceful love for another human being. It also reflects hope. When we pray for something, we visualize it. We imagine it. We think about how it might come about as a reality. This gesture involves mind, heart, and soul, as all parts of our being attentively wait for some answer or wisdom. When it comes, we recognize it because we have been so present, even if the answer itself does not emerge as we thought it would.

I pray for clean water in the region where my friends live in Tanzania. Water must be boiled for hours or otherwise purified to be used for drinking or even bathing. It is boiled over fires that require chopping down trees to make charcoal. To travel by foot to bring the water in buckets and carry firewood requires hours each week. In my prayers, I imagine a clean water supply. I imagine what people would do with the extra time. I imagine the environmental improvements that come with less tree-cutting and fires. I imagine people would have time for education or developing other daily living skills. I imagine them learning new things and getting better jobs. I imagine they could send their children to school with greater ease. I imagine they could contribute to the life of their town or village in new ways. I imagine less disease and better health for all. This is what I hold out when I pray for clean water. Allow yourself to imagine something that fully in prayer and see what happens.

Healthy Christian communities do not exist only for themselves. They practice relationship both internally and externally. They recognize that their relationships with one another can engender spiritual health and empower them to seek justice. Grace is not just a theological term, after all; it is action on behalf of God in the world. While churches sometimes inflict damage, they are also agents of love, cherishing, social action, justice, service to the poor, and helping society be mindful and attentive to the social ills of our time. All this comes out of deep awareness of relationship and prayer for those with whom we are connected.

Return to the Spiritual Practice of Relationship

Some relationships are easy, some are challenging; they all require attention. With this spiritual practice we begin by acknowledging the humanity of another. Notice people as you pass them on the street. Greet each person you see from the moment you wake until your day is done, and offer each one reverence. Be creative in the practice and try to place people at ease. Discover ways of being in graceful communion with another if just for a moment. More complex relationships—with individuals, family members, or in a church you are considering joining—can raise your anxiety. In these cases, commit to the relationship just sixty seconds at a time. If you fail in one minute, another one will be right behind it. You can try to be more graceful in that next minute. Imagine your capacity for being present to another expanding. Imagine being the embodiment of grace with your closest friends and family and with strangers in the community.

Wondering Questions

Notice where you feel most connected to God and others. Where are the simple places for the spiritual practice of relationships? Where are the difficult ones?

What difference would it make to find a community where you could practice relationship with others?

What aspect of Christian community is, or appears, nourishing to you? Which part is, or seems, challenging to you?

Have you ever had someone pray for you or prayed for someone? How did it feel? Would you like it to happen?

CHAPTER 6

Religion Is the Story, Speaking with Your Life Is the Practice

"I want to learn everything I can about the vineyard. There is a lot of wisdom there. Really, it's a metaphor for life."

—Robin Dodd, Pessagno Winery,
Monterey County, California

That's My Story and It's Sticking to Me

Robin Dodd has a complex tattoo on his arm. It is a tree with two images of robins in it, one a bird and the other Robin Hood. There are numerous symbols among the intertwining branches that reflect his life. He meditates daily on the imagery and seeks to spiritually explore and commit to his being and purpose. The tattoo in a way has become an expression of a personal religion. It speaks a story that conveys a worldview in which he believes and seeks to live more deeply. It is not institutional. It does not demand allegiance to anyone but himself. It will not kick him out if he does not behave. It simply displays a story in which Robin finds deeper meaning and can connect his inner life to the world.

While we may not tattoo it on our arm, we all have a worldview that is exclusively ours. It relates to our unique life circumstances and the cultural context in which we are formed. It shapes our commitments and sense of purpose, what we believe and how we behave. It is, in a way, our religion.

On the day I wrote this, Wikipedia defined religion as "a collection of cultural systems, belief systems, and worldviews that relate humanity to spirituality and, sometimes, to moral values. Many religions have narratives, symbols, traditions, and sacred histories that are intended to give meaning to life or explain its origin or that of the universe. They tend to derive morality, ethics, religious laws, or a preferred lifestyle from their ideas about the cosmos and human nature. According to some estimates, there are roughly 4,200 religions in the world."[21]

---

21 http://en.wikipedia.org/wiki/religion

By all sociological accounts, the perceived cultural purpose of religion in the West is changing. Harvey Cox suggests that it is moving toward a "rediscovery of the sacred in the immanent, the spiritual within the secular. . . . People turn to religion more for support in their efforts to live in this world and make it better, and less to prepare for the next."[22]

Cox's way of conveying the role of religion is more responsive to the spiritual hunger in our culture today. Historically, spirituality has been a subset of religion. From its cultural roots (and in the West this was the religious home of spirituality), a duality developed between the spiritual and the physical world. The spiritual world was seen as superior. Hierarchies developed in both realms. This worldview in turn undergirded patriarchal religion. For example, the body was of less value than the mind and spirit, certain bodies and sexual expressions were less valuable than others, and some were just considered inhuman.

It may be that the emphasis on spirituality without religion in our culture is a rejection of such dualisms. We now search for new frameworks that suit this day and age, where people tend to think in terms of relationality rather than hard and fast polarities. Informed by science and new perspectives on social justice, the hierarchical religious structures that previously dominated political and social discourse make less sense to many people. Including many religious people.

While some would consider the lessening of religious influence as a positive development, I wonder if we have not thrown the baby out with the bathwater. I am not sure, for instance, we have a handle on how we effectively integrate our spiritual selves into our materialistic world. Generally speaking, as a culture, we still polarize physical and spiritual life. Spiritual tourism, secular spirituality, and consumer spirituality are on the rise. Excessive self-pleasing habits leave us in poor physical and spiritual health. Concerns for our personal satisfaction now

---

22 Cox, 2.

dominate, and spirituality unfortunately seems to end up as a subset not of religion but of consumer culture. We are obviously unsatisfied with material things and looking for—but having difficulty finding—something more. Ursula King has a sense of what we seek. She writes:

> Contemporary understandings of spirituality capture the dynamic, transformative quality of spirituality as lived experience, an experience linked to our bodies, to nature, to our relationships with others and society. It is an experience which seeks the fullness of life—a life of justice and peace, of integrating body, mind, and soul, a life that touches the hem of the spirit in the midst of all our struggles of living in a world that has become ever more globally interdependent, yet is so painfully torn apart.[23]

If this is what we spiritually seek, we might still find it in a religious tradition. But the average person joining an organized religion today needs to know their own story is included in the broader narrative of that religion. If the tradition cannot offer a place for one's personal narrative, if they have to subjugate their story (or their freedom) to a religious cultural tradition that makes no sense to them, then they are not likely to try to make it their spiritual home.

The measure by which religions are assessed could now be, "Does the religion provide space for the fullness of my story?" This brings us to one of the hardest questions with which individuals and religious institutions alike must wrestle: what do I do with the baggage—my own and that embedded in the institution—that limits me truly integrating my story with the story of God in a faith tradition?

23 Ursula King, *The Search for Spirituality: Our Global Quest for a Spiritual Life* (Katonah, NY: Blue Bridge Books, 2008), 3.

Jesus spoke these words. Sit with them for awhile.

He put before them another parable: "The kingdom of heaven may be compared to someone who sowed good seed in his field; but while everybody was asleep, an enemy came and sowed weeds among the wheat, and then went away. So when the plants came up and bore grain, then the weeds appeared as well. And the slaves of the householder came and said to him, 'Master, did you not sow good seed in your field? Where, then, did these weeds come from?' He answered, 'An enemy has done this.' The slaves said to him, 'Then do you want us to go and gather them?' But he replied, 'No; for in gathering the weeds you would uproot the wheat along with them. Let both of them grow together until the harvest; and at harvest time I will tell the reapers, collect the weeds first and bind them in bundles to be burned, but gather the wheat into my barn.'"

Then he left the crowds and went into the house. And his disciples approached him, saying, "Explain to us the parable of the weeds of the field." He answered, "The one who sows the good seed is the Son of Man; the field is the world, and the good seed are the children of the kingdom; the weeds are the children of the evil one, and the enemy who sowed them is the devil; the harvest is the end of the age, and the reapers are angels. Just as the weeds are collected and burned up with fire, so will it be at the end of the age. The Son of Man will send his angels, and they will collect out of his kingdom all causes of sin and all evildoers, and they will throw them into the furnace of fire, where there will be weeping and gnashing of teeth. Then the

righteous will shine like the sun in the kingdom
of their Father. Let anyone with ears listen!"
(Matthew 13:24–30, 36–43)

The farmers I learned from plucked every weed in sight
from the fields where their good seeds had been so carefully
sown. Workers search them out, moving carefully row by row,
gently pulling out the small weeds by hand, never upsetting the
plant they want to grow. Such laborers do not let weeds take
root near a head of lettuce, or even a grapevine, which seems
too large to be affected by a little weed. Even with the method
of broadcast seeding, where seed is scattered rather than sown,
the sudden infusion of weeds in this story must have come as a
shock; for surely the laborers in the first century were as diligent
as those of today.

On the other hand, not all weeds are menacing to a fruitful
harvest. Some make for good pest control, inviting consumption
of the weed instead of the fruit-bearing plant. Others are nox-
ious, poisonous, or in some way a deterrent to a bug. In any case,
the rapid and strong growth of the weeds we see in this parable
seems to make it a bad harvest decision to pull them out at this
advanced stage. To eliminate the weeds is to lose the wheat. As
we have learned from our other parables, the harvest itself is of
primary concern.

Another reality of modern-day farming is that sometimes too
much product is grown and the farmers cannot afford to harvest
the excess. Their contracts are for a certain amount of lettuce,
but they plant more just in case. They literally have to "disc,"
or chop up, some of the crop and leave it in the field to fertilize
the soil for the next planting. It is not wasted, but returns to the
ground as useful nourishment for the next crop. While fertilizing
is good, they might also give the produce away, but agricultural
regulations (in California at least) are so strict they cannot let
just anyone into the fields to glean them, and they cannot afford
to harvest and deliver the product to a food bank.

This is the big picture decision for the farmer. The laborers lament that "their" lettuce never makes it to our dinner tables. They have nurtured it, kept the weeds and every other menace out of the fields, only to not harvest the fruit of their labor. These heads of lettuce have grown synergistically, side-by-side for an entire season. Each head is a product of their care and collaboration. But everyone must submit to the wisdom of the one who has ultimate responsibility. In the end, the farmer must make the decision that is best for the harvest.

Our parable serves as a spiritual and religious metaphor on a number of levels. The text itself was written at a time when dualistic modes of thought were the norm. Interpretations of texts such as these have quite literally been used to put the fear of God in people in order to garner their commitment to the Christian faith (no one wants to be a weed thrown into the furnace of fire, and many are wary of a religion that proposes such a fate). For those of us making sense of the universe with a less dualistic mindset, we struggle with such limited thinking. Especially when it comes from Jesus himself.

The Christian hope, however, is that God will redeem the universe; that is, God will heal and properly order all things according to God's loving plan. This may mean that in the end, some things will need to be transformed. Ash, after all, is excellent fertilizer for the earth. Beautiful, healthy, fruit-bearing plants usually "shine like the sun" when emerging from the effort that has gone into making rich soil.

Rather than focus on the separation and punishment of one group of people and the salvation of a chosen few, I see something else at work in this parable. While there may be thoroughly evil people that just need to go, we can also consider the weeds not as the whole person, sinners and "evildoers," but the impulses within each of us and in our world that resist God. Rooting these out can be a painful process, in itself, and one we are likely to resist. We are bothered by the death of something within ourselves. Ask anyone who has been through detox. We lament when even something detrimental that needs to die in our lives does indeed die. We wail and gnash our teeth. We grieve deeply in our letting go.

On the level of individual spirituality, we might long for God to reorder our personal lives. For those things in our lives that are out of our control, things we cannot seem to change, there is the promise that one day they will be settled by a presence and power external to our own. There will be transformation. No more daily overcoming of our addiction, darkness, struggles, persecutions, and injustices. We will be completely free of those things that are a constant source of pain and which we cannot seem to change no matter how we try. We will be in the kingdom, and it will be pure and sweet.

On the institutional level, we also long for transformation. Christianity has often been caught up in the growth of the institution more than the growth of the faith. It has invested in reinforcing the culture and reigning authorities. As a result, institutional Christianity has usually supported the patriarchal and colonizing forces that controlled so much of Western life. The domestication or annihilation of vibrant and diverse peoples has been a part of the intertwining of culture and religion. Amidst the multitude of good things Christianity has accomplished, we have "weeds" that need to go into the fire.

The church can and should work for change and bring justice where we are able, within our institutional life and beyond. But there is also a time for patience and recognition that sin, pain, and injustice dwell in our midst and are part of our story. It is inevitable that both "wheat" and "weeds" make up the fullness of who we are. In these insurmountable places where we cannot seem to overcome, we pray for God's wisdom and strength to redeem the whole creation. In church sometimes we say, "Come, Lord Jesus, come!" In such words we express the error of our ways on a grand scale, our powerlessness to redeem ourselves, and our trust in God to bring the kingdom in its fullness.

If we trust that this all-powerful God is also gracious and all-loving, can we trust that God will order our individual and communal lives with justice and grace? Can we trust that in the letting go, a better life will emerge? Can we place our stories and our lives in the hands of God?

The Christian promise is a hope-filled one grounded in the faith that all things can be redeemed and will work out in the end for good, for the kingdom of God. It is broad, deep, and marked by a grace that encompasses all. In this larger story, the stories of many individuals could find a home.

In the Meantime

Christianity began as a movement, not a religion or an institution. It was a collection of people who pursued spiritual wisdom through Jesus and developed community around his presence. They wished to devote their lives to this graceful way. The values derived from this experience guided how they lived.

Part of their context was a belief that the end of the world was imminent. Christians understood this to mean that God's kingdom would come and God's order for the world would prevail. They sought to live in such a way that they were ready for this transition; not only for themselves but so others could know it and also be ready.

Early Christians experienced great persecution, and eventually a close-knit community with a well-defined identity began to emerge. The duality of "us and them" thinking delineated who would pass muster in the end times and who would not. While this was the mindset of the time, certainly it remains today; we still fall into such dualistic ways of ordering our worldview. Isn't there that certain someone you would just love to kick out of your life?

As time passed, and the world changed but did not end, communities of disciples adjusted accordingly. They developed local interpretations of the story and the teachings of Jesus. Theologies began to form, and community lifestyles and behavior patterns took root, intertwining with those of the wider culture. What was a movement shifted into a way of being in the world known as Christian. The New Testament writings reflect these developments, including the conflicts that naturally occur amidst any group of people living together. Christianity, then, continued to form a culture of its own.

There was probably less uniformity in theology and culture than we imagine when Christianity finally institutionalized. In the fourth century the battle over doctrine or "right belief" was settled in the Council of Nicea, under the power of the Emperor Constantine. It established an official and orthodox position for the basic beliefs and tenets of Christianity. Life on the theological margins surely continued, but there was now a distinct and dominant voice in control.

I Like Beige, Just Not All the Time

Part of the story of Christianity, then, is that it became an institution. The nature of institutionalization is to create an average, a norm, out of a broad spectrum of experience. This happens with religion and every other type of institution, and it is not always bad. Uniform ways of doing things and common beliefs and behaviors are necessary to well-functioning, large communities. Institutions can offer a broad place of belonging, and legitimate rites of passage such as birth, marriage, and death. They can speak powerfully for the body on justice issues, and take collective action on behalf of individuals who cannot speak for themselves.

Institutions can be very important in the life of any community. We do need them.

Institutions as the only voice of faith, however, can discourage the spiritual power that is present in our individual stories. An institution generally ignores or diminishes the margins because they deviate from the preferred norm or pose a threat to the mainstream. Institutions operate in ways that paint in large broad strokes, leaving out detail, nuance, and color. Before you know it, everything looks the same. Sameness is much easier to manage than diversity. Crowd control is sensible for an institution, but over time vibrancy can be lost. The institution can come to exist only for itself.

Another way of picturing this is to literally picture the color beige. It is a fine wall color for a decorated room. To see the light of beige, though, other deeper colors need to be present. In paintings, beige is more often a highlight than a backdrop. Its lack of color can delineate color, set things apart, but on its own, it highlights nothing. Beige is fine, just not everywhere all the time. Institutions should serve as a backdrop, a container, to hold the vibrancy of the life they are meant to serve. They are not the fullness of life themselves. Local culture, for example, should be reflected in a community's worship life, alongside the institutional identity with which the church is affiliated.

In the absence of that cultural color, blandness can take over and trickle inward to our spiritual experience of God. God can become boring, beige, if we only experience God through the institution. Imagine that: the creator of heaven and earth as a boring being! The God of the scriptures is hardly that. The God of the scriptures can be erratic, fierce, wildly and erotically loving, scary, passionate, deeply intimate, creative, and deadly. But never boring.

Yet those who become accustomed to their institutional story can cease to experience awe, joy, and humility at the miracle of creation. We don't really expect God to make a miracle in our lives, let alone notice when God actually does. We read scripture unmoved by its spiritual truth, appalling violence and injustice, as well as ignoring the mirror it provides for the fullness of the human/divine story. People who have gone to church for a long time can easily shrug their shoulders when hearing of the transformation Jesus brought to so many. We can take for granted or brush past the stunning implications of the resurrection.

We can also become numb to the very suffering Jesus sought to alleviate. We cast a suspicious eye on the thousands who formed faith communities in those early days, and on others who follow in ways that do not resonate with our own. Our Christian story gets bland and rationalized down to something quite small, lacking any sense of wonder and imagination. The institution can mindlessly drone on to the point that we yawn and grow content to listen to what we have always heard but not really engage.

As Christianity emerges to a new self in this postmodern age, we need all our stories of longing and of transformation to be heard. Exploiters and the exploited, margins and center, all need to speak and to listen to one another. It is unfortunate that the stories of the margins and alternative modes of sharing Christianity have not always come to the fore. It impoverishes spiritual depth for us all.

For instance, Western culture encourages us to speak more than we listen, and that speech can take on a dogmatic and dominant tone. Speaking well and shutting down other voices is how we attain power in America. This does not always allow for the diverse stories of all who inhabit our world to be heard. To expand the repertoire of faith stories that lead us into a deeper and grace-filled transformation, we must take time to listen to them. We must take time to discern and speak our own.

People who describe themselves as spiritual tell sociologists that they struggle to find a church where their inner life can be vibrantly and meaningfully expressed. In other words, when they go to church, they do not always find there a place for the inclusion of their spiritual story. They find the church more focused on its institutional life than on the world around it. If this is your experience, you are not wrong. The church often speaks only to itself. The stories of the "spiritual but not religious," those with no affiliation and anyone not schooled in institutional faith life, may not be seen or heard.

What would it look like for the church to listen to a greater diversity of voices? To expand its faith-sharing repertoire beyond proclamation? Perhaps we could converse instead of debate with those who desire spirituality but who do not live in the world of religion. If you are a person of faith now, how would you tell your colorful, vibrant, and transforming story in a way that a person outside the church might hear it? If you are exploring Christianity, how could you best share your vibrant story of God (or not God) as you understand it? How would we need to behave with each other for this to happen?

Difficult as this work may seem, fear not and do not lose hope! The liberating news of grace always manages to slip through our greatest failings. To me, that is the good news. Grace always shows up. People of diverse backgrounds, on all sides of a power equation, have managed to see miracles, to experience the power of resurrection, to follow the graceful way with their heart, mind, and soul despite human failing. We live the story, not because an institution told us to, but because the story lives in us.

The Spiritual Practice of Speaking with Your Life

The other spiritual practices discussed in this book are not uniquely Christian. Speaking the Christian story with your life is. It is the practice of sharing a story with Christ; that is, living in Christ and allowing Christ to live in you. When we commit to Jesus and his graceful way, together, we become a story. The main way we enter that story is through baptism. Like a tattoo it is permanent. Baptism is not henna dye that wears away and needs to be renewed—or not. Baptism is the indelible image of the constant presence of Christ in our lives. Although my interpretation of life in Christ is free to change, the image remains for my whole life.

The spiritual practice of speaking your life happens as you develop your inner story and express it into the world. This is how we become the story. If you are baptized or considering it, imagine the permanent aspects of the Christian life that you hope to always express. What essence of your life in Christ would you "tattoo" on your arm to reflect your faith and values into the world?

One of the most important steps in living out this practice is finding a Christian community that encourages your journey, a

safe place where you can express grace into the world in a meaningful way. In other words, part of this practice is to discern the
local church or other community where your spiritual story can
be fully present.

As previously noted, Christianity is a communal faith, based
on a communal understanding of a loving God. People who
commit to faith in baptism make a commitment to God in Christ
and the universal church, but live it out locally. They receive support from a local and a wider church; the institution that enables
their journey and helps them to see how their story fits into the
greater one. In my own faith tradition, we say these words after
a baptism:

> Heavenly Father, we thank you that by water
> and the Holy Spirit you have bestowed upon
> this your servant the forgiveness of sin, and
> have raised them to a new life of grace. Sustain
> them, O Lord, in your Holy Spirit. Give them
> an inquiring and discerning heart, the courage
> to will and to persevere, a spirit to know and to
> love you, and the gift of joy and wonder in all
> your works.[24]

What wonderful words to hear as you begin the spiritual
practice of speaking the story with your life. This is what the
local community facilitates. We worship, pray, study, serve,
and have fun together. We live into this prayer daily; for living
in grace means there will be something new to learn each day
about this essence of God. Many people find church to be a sort
of surrogate family, especially in a culture where biological families are not always close. Our church family and friends may be
the community where we practice and are encouraged in what
it means for us to have an "inquiring and discerning heart, the
courage to will and to persevere, a spirit to know and to love
[God], and the gift of joy and wonder in all God's works." We

---

24 The Book of Common Prayer, 308.

then take the fruit of those relationships into our daily lives and share them with our presence. Such outward signs of our inner life become, if you will, a tattoo of the faith that we embody in our world.

Becoming Icons

Icons are not just works of art, but "windows into heaven," as they are sometimes defined. They colorfully depict the story of saints, Mary the mother of Jesus, Christ himself, or God the Trinity. Orthodox churches are filled with icons that tell the story using images instead of words. The intent is to draw the viewer beyond the image and more deeply into the mystery of God so we can know our life with God.

An elderly Russian woman was asked how the faith of many Russian Orthodox followers of Jesus survived—and even thrived—during the Soviet period when Christians were persecuted. The woman replied, "They could teach us atheism, tear down the churches, forbid us from worshipping, but we always had the icons. . . ."[25] While churches and religious buildings were destroyed, icons were hidden and smuggled out of Russia by the hundreds. The Eastern practice of using icons to see beyond the physical sustained and even deepened their faith through torturous times.

As we grow and develop spiritually, our lives can become icons for someone else to gaze upon. Someone may experience God through you and your story. They may look at your life and see something deeper in their own. Such an insight could change everything.

Christianity, in some places a marginalized cultural icon or even a relic, in other places a dualistic system in dire need of internal transformation, is still the bearer of a story that is a sacred and historic reality. Christians, who make up the body of

---

25 An Israeli tour guide, Usama Salman, shared this legend with me as she discussed the numerous icons smuggled into the regions of the Holy Land during the Marxist era.

Christ, the church, help people look through the story to discover life with God. Both individually and corporately, we help people imagine living in a Christian framework that becomes a place for their own story to find a home. This is the spiritual practice of people who have committed to a faith life.

Whether the institutional life of the church is big and booming or not, Christians need to understand themselves as icons. Indeed, given the weeds that have grown up within and around Christianity, we may be in a period of history where these smaller, more personalized windows into the rich life of Jesus Christ are a more effective witness to grace. How could your life—your story—become just such an icon? Or for a more contextual metaphor, how would a tattoo the length of your arm reflect your life in Christ?

Return to the Spiritual Practice of Speaking with Your Life

Speaking the Christian story with your life is a unique Christian practice. It is the practice of living one's identity in the faith of Christ in such a way that the world can see—showing the tattoo of your faith and knowing that it guides you and inspires others. Living intentionally within a particular framework gives us depth of understanding of our place in the world and how to live. Faith guides our living in an integrated way.

This practice depends on finding a community where you can live your story in the context of the greater story. As we keep our commitments to the life of grace, as we serve others and pursue justice, we tell a story that reveals God's life to the world.

Wondering Questions

Where in your life do things need "rooting out and burning up"?

What are the parts of other people or religious traditions that you tend to judge? What would it feel like to release some of that judgment?

If you are new to faith, what would it be like to commit to Jesus, join a faith community, be baptized, and bind your story with the Christian story? If you are already baptized, could you recommit to your faith on a deeper level?

How could you better articulate your faith story? How could you tell it with your life? If you were going to create a tattoo on your arm with symbols that reflected your spiritual life and values, what would it look like?

How could you become a better listener to others' stories? How could your personal narrative benefit from theirs?

Final Thoughts

Even our questions are praise to God's ears.

A woman came to me after church one day, tears in her eyes, reassured by the sermon she had heard that day. I had simply said that I thought questions were a normal part of a healthy spiritual life. She was worried that questions were a sign of atheism. She was not sure what she wanted, but she knew atheism was not her path. My words affirmed for her that she was not an atheist. I was glad to be of service.

Questions are an important part of life. We all know this, but having the courage to ask them can be a challenge. We can feel insecure. We have been taught that it is best to have all the answers and be able to defend our point of view. We are often expected to know more than we do or at least to be completely confident in the knowledge we have acquired. To ask for information can sometimes feel intimidating. We should already know. This happens regularly in religious contexts.

I am of the opinion that questions are good, and not only to produce the answer we already know is right. I would like to embrace other uses of questions, such as to inspire wonder. My father-in-law is an engineer. My husband has the same kind of mind. They both will look at something mechanical or that otherwise has moving parts and, like clockwork, they will ask: "How does that work?" They don't already know the answer. They stare at things, and furrow their brows, and turn the object over in their hand if they can. They ponder. They wait. They know that part of the joy of discovery is the process of wondering. It may take awhile—days or months—to get an answer. Scientists spend years asking questions about how things work, how they could work. They have one question that leads them to a thousand more, that helps them make one stunning, life-changing discovery. Are we not grateful for their ability to ask questions that have no predetermined answer?

Questions that help us wonder help us discover God. Dialogue especially includes questions, not to get at predetermined truths, but because we are curious to truly know another and be known in the discourse. Taking our stories and allowing them to join and become a shared story is where community happens. Faith is born in the places where truth is not understood as finite, but where seeking and finding is a relaxed and natural part of life. And even if we think truth is finite, like scientists, could we take the approach in matters of spirituality and faith that there is always more to learn? And that there are as many languages and ways to express that truth as there are people to share it?

That is the journey I hope we have shared in these pages. I pray reading this book and pondering questions with me have enriched your spiritual journey. I pray that it has drawn you to new questions and a new confidence about your own wisdom, so that you can walk farther on your path. I pray that you find and help create a place of dialogue for matters of spirituality and faith. I pray that the grace of God has enlarged your life and that you have discovered fresh awareness, healing, joy, and deep peace.

And I pray you will have courage and speak something of your spiritual story. It is a gift to be shared.

Printed in the USA
CPSIA information can be obtained
at www.ICGtesting.com
JSHW021547200124
55758JS00002B/3